For Whom THE LIGHT Beckons

Moments *of* LIGHT
Moments *of* TRUTH
GEMS *for* Contemplation

by G O D
in Communion with
Lawrence Hall Dawson

Copyright ©2006 All Rights Reserved.
ISBN 1-59405-078-3
Cover design, John Wayne Eastwood.
Reproduction in any medium without written
consent of the author is expressly prohibited.
Published by N2Print.
Published and Printed in the United States of America.

"Restive hearts
be at Peace…
as this testifies
The TRUTH
of thy Beingness."

Preface

These "Moments of LIGHT – Moments of TRUTH: GEMS for Contemplation" entitled *For Whom the Light Beckons*, have been compiled by Lawrence Hall Dawson and are excerpted, quoted passages Received as Responses to questions Asked of God Mind during Communion. Many of these passages may be found within his larger volume of writings, *Return to TRUTH*; the remainder, however, are unpublished excerpts from his Communion.

His earlier volume, *The WAY Back Home...*, and this latest literary work, the anthology *For Whom THE LIGHT Beckons*, have as their core-focus The Understanding necessary to aid those minds of humankind that Desire to "Return Home to Parent Mind, God Mind."

Author's Note: *Mind* as used in this anthology, has several definitions: GOD Mind = God, Spirit, Divine Mind or Universal Mind, Allah, Great Spirit, etc.; INDIVIDUALIZED MIND-IN-SEPARATION FROM GOD MIND = soul, "lost but not forgotten"; INDIVIDUALIZED MIND IN AT-ONEMENT WITH GOD MIND = Christ, Spirit, Holy Spirit, Atman, Adibuddha, etc.

The Beacon

"Bring The Light of *TRUTH*
from under the darkness of hiding
unto
The Beacon of The TRUTH-Sayer."

To the Reader

May the reader consider the premise that humankind, as originally Created is an intrinsic part of Eternal Mind and is *not* the temporal body that it impermanently occupies. However, because of its encapsulation within a temporal body, this Mind of humankind has forgotten Its Birthright as a part of the larger mind, Parent Mind; has forgotten Its Birthright as the Offspring of this Parent Mind; has forgotten Its Birthright as The Christ.

It is the hope that the reading of *For Whom THE LIGHT Beckons* will cause you, the Prodigal Children of your Parent-in Heaven, to find your Way back Home to your TRUE Identity; to your TRUE Inheritance; to your Remembered Perfection.

Author's note: Throughout the content of this anthology, please be cognizant of the stylistic use of capitalization of those words that have a Spiritual connotation. This use of capitalization will save countless words of definitional explanatory testimony.

❁

Such are the Words of God
as Revealed through me –
not by me – but through me…

—Lawrence Hall Dawson

TABLE OF CONTENTS

Preface v
To the Reader vii
Apocalypse 1
At-Onement/Christ 9
Choice/Will 49
Communion 77
Creation (by God) 107
Creation (by Humankind) 121
Death 125
Faith 135
God 143
Guidance 155
Healing 163
Heaven 171
Hell 181
Humankind 187
Illusion/Separation 193
Peace 213
Prayer 219
Salvation/Second Coming 229
Sin/Evil 247
Trust 259

Truth	265
Amen	277
Epilogue	281
Biography	283
List of Titles	285

For Whom THE LIGHT Beckons

Apocalypse

(See also SALVATION/SECOND COMING)

Prophecy

"Prophesied as
'World Apocalypse,'
*The End of the world
of individualized mind-in-separation
from God Mind*
will Occur
as each mind-in-separation from God Mind
Weds *with* God Mind
In Wholly Matrimony, Wholly Communion."

Wait-and-See

"'Wait-and-see patterns'
of prophecy fulfillment
become the verification process
of prophecy fulfillment
of individualized mind."

Prophecies

"The prophecies *of* individualized mind
testify Truth *or* error
only after the prophecies were to have occurred!

"Received Prophecies *from* God Mind
are Testified God Mind
and
need not time to evidence their Truth."

❂

The Flood (1)

"Prophecy of the all-encompassing 'Flood'
was Testified by Noah
as Tome from God Mind
Testifying *The Spiritual Rebirth*
of individualized mind-in-separation from God Mind
Leading to Death of error."

❂

The Flood (2)

"'The Ark'
symbolized
The Christ,
The Light Body of individualized mind,
The Temple of God-in-Mind."

The Flood (3)

*"At-Onement of individualized mind
with God Mind
was symbolized by
'the Animals'
Yielding their duality
As They Reclaimed Their Inheritance."*

❂

The Flood (4)

*"'Noah'
symbolized
those individualized minds
which were Ready to do this Reclaiming."*

❂

The Flood (5)

*"'Islands rising out of the flood'
symbolized
those individualized minds
which testified lack-of-Readiness
in Reclaiming their Inheritance."*

The Flood (6)

"'Olive Branch'
symbolically Testified
*The Return of Peace
to those individualized minds
which chose to Reclaim their Inheritance.*"

❊

The Flood (7)

"'The Dove'
symbolized
*Individualized Mind in At-Onement
with
God Mind.*"

❊

The Flood (8)

"'The dry land Reappearing'
symbolized
*The Thirst for Truth
Indigenous to those individualized minds in
Separation from God Mind.*"

The Flood (9)

*"'Mount Ararat'
upon which The Ark came to rest
symbolically Represented
Kingdom-in-Heaven."*

At-Onement/Christ

(See also CREATION (by God)/Heaven)

The Cycle

"'Non-Totality'
is concept testified
by mind-in separation *from* God Mind."
Fettered by such belief,
these minds Sought to Understand
The Meaning of Life,
and in this Search
discovered the commonality of Cyclic Phenomena:
'In that which was CAUSED,
created an EFFECT,
and for EFFECT to continue,
CAUSE needs to continue also.'"

❂

Rod and Staff

"Yea, I AM
with thee Always.
As ye Step Forth
into The Light,
My Rod and My Staff,
They Comfort thee
all the days of thy life."

No Boundaries

"Individualized Mind
United *with* God Mind
will Know no boundaries;
LOVE and LIGHT
shall Follow thee
all the days of thy life,
Yea,
even unto Eternity."

Way Back Home

"'Way back Home'
is
through Remembering thy Birth
as Perfect Idea
in God Mind."

The Stick

"Testifying the Affirmation,
'I and my Father are One,'
will Remove
the stick from thine eye."

WITH TRUTH ONLY

"The 'Seeing'
is with Truth only,
not a sensory seeing.

"Offspring of Light –
The Light Body –
Knows only Its Own!
The non-sensory Light Body
is The ALL-Knowing Body,
Manifested of Light;
It is Truth-Incorporeality!"

❂

I AM

"I Am
That 'I AM'.
Think It;
Know It';
Be Its Perfect Reflection.
Begin
all Descriptions of thy BEINGness
with
That 'I Am.'"

Darkness Lifted

"A darkness
will be Lifted
from mind's soul
upon Remembering
its Divine Birthright."

❂

Move Aside

"Move aside
o' individualized mind,
make Way for Mind of God…
My mind Desires Manifestation
only of its Higher Self."

❂

Emptying

"'In Emptiness,
there is Fullness' –
'In Emptying Self
of "self,"
there remains Self only.'"

Testifying

"Denying self,
Defined God Mind,
Is 'Yielding will of individualized mind
to
Will of God.'

"Taking up The Cross,
Defined God Mind,
Is 'Yielded will Testifying Sonship.' "

❋

Christ Within

"The God-in-Mind
is
'The Christ Within,
The Son of God,
Receiver of ALL That Is.'"

❋

Within

"It is *within* the Light Body
that individualized mind
Becomes
The Perfect Reflection of God Mind
*without conscious thought
of individualized mind.*"

Fear

"Oneness
of Mind
Knows
no fear."

❊

The Ocean

"Be
'as a Drop
in The Ocean
of God Mind'
by
Yielding they will
to God's Will."

❊

Beingness

"Visualize thy BEINGness
within an Ocean,
Becoming ONE
with The Ocean."

The Path

"Way of TRUTH
is
Way of ONENESS,
The Path
to absence of separation."

❊

Separation

"As individualized mind,
Attract
absence of separation
from God Mind."

❊

Allness

"ONE is ALL;
therefore,
Understand: thou art ONE
with The ALL.

"ALL is ONE;
therefore, that which is done
to the least of My Children
is done to The ALL."

God Is

"Only God IS!
No other goes before God.
From Perfection
Comes Perfection.

"The individualized mind
which Joins The Father
in ALL-encompassing LOVE
will Know only Perfection."

Return

"Understand,
o' individualized mind,
thou art Made
in My Image
and after My Likeness;
It is Mind of God Playing upon Itself,
Harmonic Convergence
of Mind upon mind."

My Pattern

"I Make all Mind
in My Image and after My Likeness;
therefore,
all Mind is in My Pattern of Perfection -
not one is not so Made.
Mind needs only Remember its Perfection."

Spirit

"When individualized mind
Yields *to* God Mind,
It is 'Spirit',
Idea-in God Mind.

"*The Spirit*
is
'God Mind *within* individualized mind,'
The Giving of God
to individualized mind."

❀

Wedding

"*WEDDING*
Defined God Mind,
Means
'to Testify WHOLENESS';
thereby Affirming
absence of duality in Mind."

❀

Embryo

"Individualized mind,
which is an Embryonic Bride
of The Bridegroom (God Mind),
is Seeking Wholly Matrimony."

Bride and Groom

"The WEDDING
of The Bride and Groom:
'Christ-in-humankind'...
Attracting
Oneness in God Mind."

Bride or Bridegroom

"When it is in Wedded Bliss
with God Mind,
Individualized Mind
Serves
The Role of 'Bride.'

"God
Testifies 'The Bridegroom,'
and
The Christ
Testifies 'The Bridegroom';
'Bridegroom' Addresses
The *Giver* Aspect of God."

CHRISTSHIP

"Not until
individualized mind-in-separation
from God Mind
WEDS
its Parent Mind, God Mind,
will such individualized minds
UNDERSTAND 'Christship.'"

❊

FORGET NOT

"Forget not
thy Inheritance as The Son of God,
as I Am
thy Father-in-Heaven.
When Wedded in Holy Matrimony,
individualized mind
with
God Mind,
this Mind is The Christ."

❊

WHOLLY MATRIMONY

"Wholly Matrimony
is
'Returning to WHOLENESS,
through
Wedding individualized mind
with
God Mind.'"

Consummation

"Individualized mind-in-separation from God Mind
is The Bride,
Inheriting ALL That Is
from The Bridegroom – God Mind –
upon Consummation of The Wedding Ceremony.

"(Consummation is to be Wholly Consumed,
The Act of 'Becoming As-One, At-One,
with The Beloved!)"

❂

Wedding

"Wedded At-Onement
sequesters humankind
as MIND
in The Bosom of God Mind,
its Parent."

❂

The Birth

"Yielding of The Bride
to The Bridegroom,
Testifies At-Onement *with* The Bridegroom
(which Manifests 'The Christ').

"Manifestation of The Christ
is The Birth of True Mind.
The Birthing –
Individualized mind's Remembrance
of its Heavenly Home."

The Birthing

"Wedding
of individualized mind
with
its Parent, God Mind,
Births
The Christ, The True Self."

❊

As Above, So Below

"ONENESS *with* The Father
is
only *through* The Christ;
therefore,
as Jesus Affirmed his Sonship
with his Father-in-Heaven,
Oneness *below*
Became
as Oneness *Above*."

❊

Single Eye

"Wedded in Oneness
individualized mind *with* God Mind –
two will Become as One
when 'Keeping thine Eye Single.'"

Birthing Reality

"Birthing Reality
is Accomplished
with At-Onement of individualized mind
with God Mind
(which Attracts the Oscillatory Frequency
of Light,
and the Yielding to these Frequencies of Oscillation,
Transcends the darkness
To Emanate The Light of Truth)."

Marriage

"That which individualized mind
labels 'marriage'
testifies *legal* wedding
of male animal body and female animal body.
Attraction of such weddings
is to legally insure conjugal rights of those so wedded."

Juxtaposing

"Understand,
weddings of animal bodies
juxtapose legal dogma
upon Offspring of God Mind –
which testifies an abomination
of God's Plan of The Returning Prodigal Child
in Oneness with The Parent.
Therefore, *Wholly Matrimony* is
'Returning to Wholeness
through Wedding
individualized mind *with* God Mind.'"

❃

Wholly/Holy Matrimony

"Understanding of Weddings
of woman and man:
'Woman and man
are but the animal bodies
of individualized mind-creation –
therefore, *illusory.*
Testifying Truth,
The Christ
Knows Wedded Oneness,
each with The ALL –
This is *Wholly/Holy Matrimony.*'"

Return

"As mind Remembers
Its Oneness *with* God Mind,
The Return to WHOLENESS will Begin."

❊

Unfoldment

"Wed thy understanding of TRUTH
with Be-Attitude
of effective, God-Directed Unfoldment."

❊

Follow

"Follow the Direction
Testified by Jesus, The Christ
when He Realized His Birthright:
'Affirm thy Sonship by Declaring,

"I and my Father are One,
not my will
but Thy Will be Done.""'"

Jesus, the Christ

"'Jesus, The Christ' – CAUSE
is Son of God
from Individualized Mind's Beginning.
(CAUSE is 'The Christ,'
The Light Body of all individualized mind.)

"'Jesus' was the name given to the receiving temple
(or animal body) during the reign of Caesar Augustus."

❁

Same

"'Christ'
is *The Light Body*
of Jesus
as It is *The Light Body*
of individualized mind;
each
Addresses 'The Christ'"

The First

"MIND of Jesus
was
'The First Individualized Mind
to incarnate *within* an animal body
AFTER ascending as The Christ,'

"This Descent
was The Demonstration of Truth
as Testified *through* The Christ,
The Revelator Angel
(Which Spoke to John in *Revelation*)."

Testified Sonship

"Jesus, The Christ,
Testified His Sonship
and so Became
the first individualized mind-in-separation
from God Mind
to Ascend
in At-Onement *with* God Mind."

Testify

"ALL individualized minds
which are in Yielded At-Onement *with* God Mind,
Testify The Christ –
The Rebirth of individualized mind-in-separation
from God Mind –
which will obviate the need
of a return to Earth-expression."

❁

Christmas Star

"Christ,
The Reflection of God Mind,
The Light Body of individualized mind,
is symbolized by
'The Christ Star'
(Testifier of At-Onement of individualized mind,
with God Mind)."

Christ Star Formation

*"As 'The Star'
is manifested symbolically,
The Oneness of individualized mind
with God Mind
is Represented by
the formation of The Star
without lifting the object of manifesting
from the surface
upon which The Star is being manifested."*

Masculine Assignation

*"God
Signifies 'Giver';
therefore,
the use of the phrase, 'The Son',
the Masculine Aspect of God (GIVING).
Life-Everlasting
is Given
through individualized mind's
'Sonship with God Mind.'"*

Non-Duality

"Individualized Mind
in At-Onement *with* God Mind
is both the *Giver* and the *Receiver*,
both the Masculine and the Feminine.

"'Son' was the label given by individualized mind
as the label for this At-Onement
with no 'correspondent' Feminine label."

※

Three as One

"'Christ'
is The Creation of God Mind,
and as such,
is The *Receiver* of ALL That is.

"Christ then Assumed 'The Perfect Image of Its Parent':
The *Giver* of Unconditioned Love."

Completion

"'Son'
is The Appellation given
Expressing Completion.
It is *through* The Son
that Life-Everlasting
is Given to individualized mind.
(This Giving is 'Son'
because Giving is the *Masculine* Aspect
of God.)"

❀

Only One

"The Light *Body*
is
The Mind 'in form' –
One MIND
One Body
in *Christ.*"

❀

Truth Testifier

"*The Christ* -
'Testifier of Truth';
'At-Onement of individualized mind *with* God Mind';
'Light Body of individualized mind';
'Atman';
'Adibuddha';
'God-in-Mind.'"

Rapture

"Rapture
Testifies
an Infilling.

"BEINGness
is Fullness –
Fullness of The Christ."

※

I Am/Thou Art

"As I AM,
thou Art –
in Perfect Reflection."

※

Attraction

"Attraction
effects
cause;
therefore,
may thy Attraction
be God
which will CAUSE
Perfect Reflection."

Atman Christ/Antichrist

"Historians
who have taken the Testimony
of Jesus, The Christ,
say,
'God is LOVE';
This is the Definition
of 'Atman Christ',
Defined God Mind.

"The *patriarchal God* (God of *fear*)
of the Old Testament –
this is the 'Antichrist'."

❊

Within/Without

"'Atman Christ'
is
The Acceptance of God Mind Within;
'Antichrist'
is
*the belief in God Mind WITHOUT
individualized mind.*"

❊

The Seed

"Mind
has 'The Seed'
of humankind's inheritance."

Nativity

"Nativity of The Christ WITHIN
is Manifested
through ONENESS of Minds:
Individualized Mind
with
God Mind."

❂

True Body

"*The Christ*
is
'humankind's True Body –
The Body of LIGHT'."

❂

Emanation

"'The Light'
of God
symbolizes
*The Radiance of Emanation
which all Light Bodies Manifest.*"

❂

The Heart

"Where thy Heart is,
there also
is The Christ."

To Be

> "'BEINGness'
> is
> GODLINESS."

❁

Wholliness

> *"Within*
> individualized mind's At-Onement
> *with*
> God Mind,
> is
> God's Wholliness."

❁

The Son

> "The SON
> is
> *in* The Father."

Oneness

"Question not
re-establishment of thy ONENESS
with thy Father-in-Heaven,...
As It WAS
IS
and
always SHALL BE."

❂

The Spiritual Heart

"Christ is Ever-Present
within *The Spiritual Hearts*
of all individualized mind;
Testifying The Sonship
of all individualized mind;
Sanctifying The Creation
of individualized mind
as The Perfect Image of its Creator,
God Mind."

Motive

"Manifestation of The Body of Christ –
The Body of Light –
Requires
Perfect Motive.

"Think not of Perfect Motive;
It Knows only Itself!"

❇

Sowing Thy Seed

"Sow thy Seed
in Straight Rows,
and
thy Harvest
shall be
PERFECT!"

❇

Narrow Way

"'Way of The Truth-Seeker'
is
The Narrow Way.
(As At-Onement of individualized mind
and
God Mind Occurs,
this is 'The Narrow Way.')"

Straightness

"Thy Way
will
be Made Straight;
be not afraid.
('Straight'
addresses
'Way of TRUTH'.)"

❊

Being Meek

"'Being Meek'
is *Yielding*,
Testifying of humankind's will
to God's Will
which will Allow individualized mind
to Inherit The ALL."

❊

To Yield

"'Yielding'
is
*to withhold all sensory and thought input
of the animal body.*"

Seeing (1)

"Yield
to Heaven-on-Earth
through
Using the Eyes of Spirit -
See *with* thine Heart."

Bliss

"Yielding
to God's Will,
Attracts individualized mind
to Heavenly Bliss –
The State of Mind
where ALL is Seen
through Eyes of Spirit.

"This Seeing
shall Reveal individualized mind
as it Truly IS."

Seeing (2)

"To See
with Spiritual Eyes,
is
to 'See The Inherent Perfection
of individualized mind';
MIND
is
Perfect."

Heaven-in-Earth

"Yielding
thy will
to
God's Will,
Causes
Heaven-*in*-Earth.
Attraction of individualized mind
shall be
to its Parent *only*."

❁

Portrayal

"*Way of The Actor*
is 'Yielding will of the Actor
to
The Will of The Playwright,'
The Creator
of The Character being Portrayed."

❁

Master

"No outer control
of the MIND of humankind
will ever be possible,
as MIND is Master to us;
we are not Master to MIND!"

True Foundation

"Our True Foundation,
that which gives us the Attraction to ALL Good,
is The Mind.

"Once Mind is accepted
as The Currency common to all,
we will attain our goal of Peace –
the goal attainable
by all
INDIVISIBLY and COLLECTIVELY."

❈

Through Me

"'No mind Comes to God
but *through* Me,' Says The Lord.
'Thy Love is My Love;
thy Joy is My Joy –
individualized mind in At-Onement *with* God Mind
is My Perfect Reflection.'

"Pursuing The Way of The Lord,
Makes individualized mind
a Fulfillment of The Attributes of God;
individualized mind *is* but an empty cup
waiting to be Infilled with The Love and Joy of God."

The Self

"LOVE
is
'thy TRUE Self' —
individualized mind
in At-Onement with God Mind."

❊

Unconditioned

"Loving *Unconditionally*
removes
the darkness of ignorance
veiling the True Self.

"Unconditioned Love
is
Seeing with Spiritual Eyes
humankind as unembodied Mind,
The Child of God Mind."

United

"Have the World
United only in Love,
and
The Author of Peace
will be God Himself!

"Our churches will not be our Salvation;
Minds United in Oneness will!"

Love Thy Neighbor

"'Love of thy neighbor'
is
to Recognize The Christ
within all individualized minds.

"'Thou shalt love thy neighbor as thyself'
Requests individualized mind
to relinquish its belief
in separation from its Parent, God Mind,
Testifying in its stead this TRUTH:
'ALL is One; ALL is Love'."

Love Is

"In Love,
no quelling of hate is manifested.
Love is forever in juxtaposition
with Oneness;
therefore,
Love Is."

Joy

"Joy
is simply The Effect
of Testifying LOVE."

❁

Reflecting Love

"'The Testifying of JOY
is the Reflecting of Love,'
Says the Lord,
'thou Become That Which I Am;
as thou Reflect The Love of God,
thou Become JOY-Manifest.'"

❁

God-in-Mind

"HARMONY –
Genesis of God-in-Mind –
is The Testimony of The Joining
of individualized mind *with* God Mind
in At-Onement.

"This At-Onement may be Accomplished
through Yielding
the will of individualized mind to God's Will."

Image

"For God so Loved Creation,
He
Gave
unto It
The Image of Himself,
and whosoever
Testifies this Image
shall have At-Onement
with God."

❂

Giving

"'*Giving* precedes *receiving*'
this is The Precept –
upon Understanding –
that provides humankind
its Growth."

❂

Give/Receive

"God
GIVES;
humankind
RECEIVES.
ALL is 'God';
therefore, individualized mind
cannot take from another
That which is God's."

The Cross

"The Cross
is individualized mind's symbol
of 'The Tree of Life.'

"Its Manifestation
is as the tree grows:
the *stem springs* forth from the earth
(or individualized mind)
and grows toward Heaven
(or God Mind).
The *branches*
symbolize the Giving-Receiving-Giving
of God-in-Mind."

Perfect Mind

(Revelation VII:4 "…were sealed an hundred and forty and four thousand…")

"The number
one hundred forty-four thousand
symbolizes 'Perfect Mind'.
(The number *twelve* symbolizes 'At-Onement';
Twelve times twelve
symbolizes
'Receivership in God Mind.')"

Inheritance

"I was Created
in His Image and After His Likeness;
therefore,
I Am Heir to His Kingdom

"Yielding my will
to God's Will
Allows my Inheritance to Manifest.
Becoming At-One *with* God
is Reclaiming my Inheritance."

❈

Perfect Pattern

"*Mind* of humankind
Recognizes Its Original Pattern of Perfection,
therefore, teach the body in which It Resides
to 'Repattern all of its sensory and thought input
so as to Image
Its Original Perfect Pattern of Oneness
with The Creator.'"

Choice/Will

Openness

"Understanding (that which is new)
will need
an Openness of Mind
as that which is new
tends to destroy
that which is old."

❋

Birhtright

"Remember
thy Birthright
as an *Offspring of God.*"

❋

No Separation

"Believe *not* in separation;
be *of the world*
but not *in the world*.

"In Mind
there is *no* separation."

SECURITY

"Security
resides in Heavenly Stewardship.
Be Cognizant of Be-Attitude
which effectively Begets
loss described as 'ego'.
Be as a Steward to thy 'True Self'."

✺

TREASURES

"Only Remember this:
ALL
is MIND,
in Truth;
therefore,
lay thy Treasures
in Heaven
not upon the Earth.

"Attraction to worldly treasures
is TEMPORAL,
but Attraction to Heavenly Treasures
is
ETERNAL."

Discretion

"Will
is
individualized mind's
'tool of discretion';
it which makes God's Will
its will,
shall Profit accordingly."

❈

Will

"WILL
wills
will
to
Manifest God's Will."

❈

The Climate

"The Climate
of today's Receivership
Affords Opportunities
for soul Growth."

Uniqueness

"Effect be-attitude of freedom
giving thyself permission
to be thy *unique* self.

"As thy *uniqueness* is testified,
thy JOY is effected.

"JOY will be effect
of living without fear."

Right Path

"The soul
Feels
its Right Path;
therefore,
Follow thine Heart."

Fear

"Cause
born with fear
will be without life."

The Gift

"ALL Life
is
'The Gift *from* God';
what humankind does
with The Gift
is
the choice of humankind."

❂

Path of Return

"Humankind
is Given
Free Will;
therefore,
each chooses the path of Return
to The Father's House;
only the soul of The Pathfinder
Knows
Its Way back Home."

The Way

"Yielding the will of humankind
to
God's Will,
is 'The Way,
The Straight and Narrow Way.'"

❂

The Journey

"*Choose*
'The Straight and Narrow Way'
and The Journey
shall not be long:
Yielding thy will always
to
God's Will."

❂

Energy-Amorphous

"Within all space
is energy-amorphous,
'clay of creation',
sentient and waiting
for 'Potters in At-Onement *with* God Mind'
or
'potters-in-separation *from* God Mind.'"

CONTROL

"The 'Power of Oneness
with God Mind'
Gives individualized mind
Absolute Control
over all of the attractions
of this world."

❁

UNFETTERED

"Create thy Kingdom-on-Earth
with Spiritual Eyes;
the *not* Seeing of God's Kingdom
through thy window
is thy choice.
Opportunities
Await thee
with Unfettered Vision."

❁

FIRST

"The *first* Birth of individualized mind
was as
'The Perfect Idea *in* God Mind.'
Yielding this Perfect Idea
of the Genesis of individualized mind
to separation of thy mind *from* God Mind,
has caused thee to leave thy *first* Love,
'God, thy Father."

Not Forgotten

"Individualized mind
made its choice
that took it
from its Place of Grace.

"From Harmony to cacophony,
sank mind from its error.

"Mind lost Sight
of its Divine Inheritance –
mind lost
but *not* forgotten."

Choice

"When the choice was made
to separate from God Mind,
Individualized Mind
became the 'soul',
lost,
but *not* forgotten!"

Re-Throning

"The de-Throning
of individualized mind
was
by choice,
and in like-measure,
The Re-Throning
of individualized mind
shall be
by choice!"

Sleeping

"Think *not*
'The Self is Conscious;
It sleeps
in The Parent Mind,
Remembering *not*
Its Inheritance
as The Son of God,
The Christ Within."

Unclaimed

"All individualized minds
have The Inheritance of God-in-Mind,
but
It remains unclaimed
by most.
Therefore,
the world
remains in darkness!"

Awaken

"Mind in Glory
Awaken to thine Inner Knowing.
It is not too late!
The Dawn of thy Rebirth
is breaking
upon Mind's darkness."

The Seed

"Created
as The Perfect Idea in God Mind,
individualized mind
is The Seed of That Perfection
with The Capabilities,
in choice,
of Becoming as The Father,
God-in-Mind.
The Embryonic God-in-Mind 'Becomes'
through these Choices."

※

To Be Like

"*IMAGE*
Signifies
'to be LIKE';
individualized mind
chooses
'to Be Like The Father'
or 'un-Like The Father';

"When individualized mind
Yields to God's Will,
It is Truly 'The Son of God Mind';
Genesis of Perfect Being
Lies in THIS Understanding."

Always

"WHOLENESS
is
individualized mind's Birthright,
past, present, future
and ALWAYS;
therefore,
Attraction to Wholeness
is ALWAYS present."

❁

Inexhaustible Supply

"Individualized mind
only Serves
as 'The Channel of LOVE Energy'.
Mind of Free Will
Accept this Divine Channeling!"

❁

The Tree of Knowledge

"'The Tree of The Knowledge
of Good and Evil'
Means
the will of individualized mind,
which knows
both Truth
and
error of individualized mind."

Future

"Future
is as clay
in the potter's hand
in a state of flux
waiting for a dream."

❂

Lost

"Individualized mind
was Given The Gift of Free Will:
to Operate in Unison *with* God Mind
or
to operate with others of like-mind,
and
individualized mind chose to play its role
with other minds of likeness of itself
and
so create a world of darkness,
and
individualized mind lost its Way."

A Way Back

"A Way back
will be Found
as each Makes The Choice to Return Home,
and then,
individualized mind will Reunite
with Mind of God.
Individualized mind will again
Take its Rightful Place
at The Right Hand of God."

❀

Rejoice

"When *The Song of Creation* is again Heard
throughout The Realm's Celestial,
all Heaven will Rejoice.
Until such Time as this Appears,
individualized mind will continue
to be mind-in-disharmony."

Symphony

"Individualized mind will again be United
with God in Co-Creation,
individualized mind *with* God Mind
Playing out a Symphonic Melody of Creation:
The Conductor
will be Mind of God;
The Orchestra
will be individualized mind –
a Symphony of The Angels of Heaven –
and The Choir,
Legions of Light.
Individualized mind will Return
in Joyful Harmony *with* its Creator."

Attraction

"A Way back may be Found
as individualized mind in At-Onement *with* God Mind
Yields to its Birthright –
an At-Onement made possible
in Mind-of-God Attraction.

"Mind has a choice:
a 'son' of individualized mind
or
a 'Son' of God.
Its Way will be Shown
on its Path of Return."

Free Will

"Our Free Will
can give us the choice:
MIND separated from Itself
or
MIND Complete Within."

Either/Or

"Humankind is MIND,
either in-separation *from* God Mind
or
in At-Onement *with* God Mind;
either / or –
these are the two choices
of individualized mind."

Two Masters

"ATTRACTION
will be
to 'the world of mind-in-separation
from God Mind'
OR
to 'The World of The Bridegroom,
Mind in At-Onement with God Mind';
humankind cannot serve two masters,
either it will deny the one
and serve the other
or compromise the both."

✦

Yielding Permanently

"Permanency
confers lack of Free Will
upon the mind of the Neophyte;
therefore,
may I Suggest
Yielding thy will
to God's Will
only when thou Desirest."

STARS

"Born of God Mind,
individualized mind
is separate *only through choice*!

"Individualized mind in At-Onement *with* God Mind
Creates 'The Christ Star';
individualized mind-in-separation *from* God Mind,
creates 'The Star of David'.
The choice is individualized mind's."

❂

WILL

"'WILL'
is humankind's Salvation
or
destruction;
the choice is humankind's alone."

❂

SERVING

"May I Suggest
not serving two masters,
as yielding to one will stay the other.
Better to Serve
thy Father-in-Heaven
than to serve
the error of individualized mind."

Tantalizing

"Segregated
into the concepts of animal body and Mind,
humankind
tantalizingly indulges
in *both* concepts simultaneously."

❁

The Mind

"The brain
is only the tool
through which the MIND works.
We *think* we are body;
we are *not*;
we are our MIND!"

❁

Vigil

"Watch thy thinking;
Keep a Vigil,
a Security Sentinel,
at the door of thy mind."

Casts Out

"Perfect Thought
casts out
perfidiousness."

❂

Serving

"Serve
one attraction:
Perfection
or
imperfection."

❂

Control

"Thinking another mind
has control over another,
is error of individualized mind.

"Each individualized mind
has God Mind *as Parent*;
therefore,
no individualized mind
can control that
to which God Mind has Given Birth."

Growth

"No mind can determine for another
HOW that mind can best Grow;
each mind
decides its own path."

❊

A Guard

"Individualized mind
needs
'to Post a Guard at its Door'
to prevent entrance of testimony
which is unlike Itself."

❊

Word Spectrum

"Word meaning energizes or de-energizes
as determined by its position
on a 'Word Spectrum'.
Those Words that Mean 'God'
are energizing;
those words that mean 'the opposite of God',
are de-energizing."

Ecology

"Think *not ecology* defines as
'the STUDY of the interrelationship
of living organisms to their environment';
think instead,
definition as
'The UNDERSTANDING of the Interrelationship
of living organisms to their environment.'"

❂

Regeneration

"*Regeneration* of nature
is only possible through Yielding
to The Universal Law of LOVE,
'As thou Givest,
so shalt thou Receivest.'"

❂

Sustaining/Maintaining

"'As nature *gives* to humankind
humankind *receives* that which was given';
therefore,
SYSTEMICALLY,
humankind needs *give back*
to Ensure Balance
of both the Giver and the Receiver."

Sanctify

"*Sanctify* the protection of the environment
by Decreeing its Beatific Correlation
to the continued existence of humankind up the Earth."

❈

No Conditions

"When Receiving from The Father *without condition*,
individualized mind is free
to do with its Gift what it desires.
'Without condition'
Defines as *no parameters*;
ALL is The inheritance of The Son of God —
individualized mind *in At-Onement
with* God Mind."

❈

Accepting

"One
either accepts fear
or Accepts LOVE;
it is the choice
of individualized mind."

Manifestation

"Giving fear expression
will attract
manifestation
of *that* fear."

❊

Yielding Not

"Yield not
to fear
My Child,
for I AM with thee
Always."

❊

Happiness

"*Cause*
Manifests
Effect;
Happiness
follows
Attraction to God Mind."

The Gift

"God
has Given individualized mind
The Gift of PERFECT IDEA;
It
needs only Accept
That Gift;
All that mind needs do
is to Affirm its Perfection –
which 'Filleth its Cup
so That it Overrunneth.'"

※

Destiny

"By Yielding
to thy Father's Will;
thy Destiny
shall be Blessed –
where thine Heart Is
so is thy Destiny."

Communion

(See also AT-ONEMENT/CHRIST)

To Eat

(Revelation II:7. "...To him that overcometh will I give to eat of the tree of life, which is in the midst of the paradise of God.")

"'To eat of the tree of life',
is
'to Commune freely with God Mind'.
This Allows
'The ONENESS with thy Father-in-Heaven' –
thy BEINGness *'in the midst of the Paradise of God.'*"

❂

Convergency

"Attraction to Heaven-World
is
'Thinking in Oneness *with* God Mind –
Testifying Testimony from God Mind
during The Communion *with* God Mind.'
This is *Convergency*."

❂

Treasures

"It is *in The Seeking
of Spiritual Understanding*,
that individualized mind
will be Able
'to Lay up its Treasures
in Heaven.'"

Gift of Tongues

"Individualized mind's True Gift of Tongues
is
Communion *with* God Mind
in The Silence."

❂

Stillness

"*Stillness*
Defined God Mind,
Means simply 'The Light';
therefore,
to Go into The Stillness is
'to Go into The Light.'"

❂

Prerequisite

"Yielding thy will
to God's Will
is Prerequisite
for Receiving TRUTH."

Belief

"Seeking Truth
is like
Seeking The Key to God's Heart;
THINK it's Possible, and
It shall be Found.
The Key is BELIEF!
(Question not 'Belief';
ye shall Know Its Presence!)"

❈

That Which I Do

"The purpose
of the churches today
is
to impart 'The Word' only –
which is perfidious –
the breaking
of the Trust
Given by Christ to His Disciples:
'This That I Do
thou canst Do also
and more.'"

The Temple

"And then
individualized mind organized the church
outside
individualized mind.
The Trust was betrayed.
'The Temple *Within*'
became
the temple *without*."

Structures, No!

"'Churches'
are
Within individualized mind,
not structures
without individualized mind
built to govern that mind."

When in At-Onement

"Individualized mind
operates
through the brain of the animal body.
This mind of humankind
when in At-Onement with God Mind
Becomes
The Holy Spirit,
Using the animal body
as 'The Church of The Living God'
on Earth."

❊

Reawakening

"Individualized minds
are being Reawakened
to The Trust
Given by Christ,
'The Trusting of individualized minds
to be Self-Determined
in Participating in Spiritual Growth.'"

Roots

"The 'Roots of Salvation'
of individualized mind-in-separation
from God Mind
Lie in The Remembrance
by individualized mind
of its Gift from The Father,
The Gift of Truth."

❂

Wholeness

"We
in Mind
will not know separation.
Give us back
The Understanding of The Return;
Give us Back
our Birthright,
and the world
will Return to Wholeness."

Beginning of the Light

"When The Desire to Know The Father
Occurs
in individualized mind,
The Receiving of The Light
will Begin –
Being in The Light
will then Commence."

❊

Accessibility

"The Parent Mind of individualized mind
is
Father to all Individualized Mind
in At-Onement *with* God Mind.

"This Fatherhood
is Accessible
to all individualized mind
which choose At-Onement."

Sustenance

"Roses seek water
for sustenance
in the same way as
Truth-Seekers Seek Truth
for Sustenance.

"Thou art a Truth-Seeker;
therefore,
I Am thy Sustenance."

❈

Desire

"When *Desire* for Communion
of individualized mind
with
God Mind Transpires,
Cause will have preceded Effect;
Manifestation of Conditions
for Perfect Receivership
will have Occurred."

Question

"'Communion'
is The Giving
of a question to God Mind
and Waiting
to Receive its Response
from 'The Mansions of Expression of God Mind'."

✺

Only Receiving, No!

"Think not Communion of individualized mind
with God Mind
is only Listening or Receiving,
as this is error-thinking.

"Communion of individualized mind
with God Mind
is first,
GIVING of the Question in The Silence Within,
followed by
Waiting upon The Lord
and Receiving The Response *from* God Mind."

Yields Upon Request

"Kingdom-in-Heaven,
the Individualized Mind in At-Onement
with God Mind,
Yields Truth
only upon Request."

✸

Interplay

"'Communion'
is to Actively Interplay
between individualized mind
and
God Mind,
beginning with a question
Asked by individualized mind
of God Mind."

✸

Readiness

"Testament of 'Readiness'
is
DESIRE only.
Desire to Commune *with* God Mind
is Testified
by 'Waiting upon The Lord'
without fear."

Ready

"Attraction *to* God Mind
Manifests
when individualized mind
is 'Ready'.
This 'Readiness' is Testified
by the Neophyte's Seeking of Answers
to Questions of Spiritual Truths."

❁

Waiting Upon

"Cause of ALL That Is,
is
God Mind.
'Waiting upon The Lord'
is
Waiting upon Cause
which Manifests Its Effect
in direct measure to that Waiting.
'Waiting'
is *Receiving Communion from God Mind*,
'Wait to Hear the Agape Voice' –
The Voice without individualized mind."

AGAPE

"'The Testifying Voice of God' –
AGAPE –
Testifies
Desire to Give *without* condition.
This is The Tenet
upon which Wisdom
is Given to all who Ask."

RECEIVED IN ONENESS

"Communion *with* God Mind
Testifies *total* Oneness
in Receiving The Testimony of God Mind.
Testimony Received in Oneness
is Truth.
Truth will be Heard *through* The Christ –
which is The Effect of Yielding
the will of individualized mind-in-separation
from God Mind
to The Will of God."

Truth Only

"Understand,
Receiving Truth only,
in Communion of thy mind *with* God Mind,
Requires
'Emptying Self of self'.
Sanctifying self
for Communion *with* thy Parent, God Mind,
Receiving of Truth
will be Assured."

Androgynous Mind

"A Time Existed
in which Androgynous Mind,
as the Undivided Mind,
Served the Dual Roles
of Teacher and Student
in Oneness."

Recreation

"The Age of Computers
is recreating
The Seedbed
and
The Climate
for the Androgynous Rejoining
of Teacher and Student Mentally.
A Return to The Oneness,
Mind as its own Inner Teacher
and its own Inner Student,
will Combine Mind's two Roles in Completeness."

❂

Analogy

"Communion *with* God Mind
following At-Onement:
This is comparable
to individualized mind being
'The Terminal Computer'
and
God Mind Serving
as 'The Master Computer Storage-Bank of ALL Truth'."

Reservoir

"The Mind of God
is
The Reservoir of TRUTH
Which Awaits
The Questioning Mind
in At-Onement *with* God Mind."

✺

The Mediator

"To Commune
individualized mind *with* God Mind
is *not* possible
without 'The Mediator',
The Light Body of individualized mind –
The Christ."

✺

The Key

"The Affirming
of The Truth of thy Inheritance,
'I Am Love,'
is *The Key*
to Allow The Prodigal Child
to Return Home."

Heart

"Where thy Heart is,
there also
is The Christ,
and
whatsoever thou shalt Ask
in My Name,
that will I Do
so that The Father
may be Glorified in the Son."

❁

The Center

"Yielding The Center
of the animal body of individualized mind,
The Heart Energy Center,
to
The Christ,
Opens 'The Door'
into thy Father's House.
(The Heart Energy Center
is The By-Word
for The Nativity of Christ.)"

The Holy Grail

"That which the Neophyte Seeks
needs only be Asked of The Father
in The Silence of the Heart –
'The Holy Grail' –
and it shall be Answered
if it be for The Highest Good
of all concerned."

❈

The Doorway

"Mind of humankind
in At-Onement *with* God Mind
is
The Doorway to Heaven."

❈

Questioning

"God
Gives to His Children
through
Questioning Hearts."

Heart Energy Center

"Since The Heart Energy Center
Testifies the Umbilical Cord
Joining The Christ –
The Light Body of individualized mind –
to
the animal body,
It is the Location
of 'The Treasure',
The Way
into thy Father's House."

❀

One

"*One* Mind, *One* Body in Christ;
therefore,
individualized mind
needs be
in Perfect Alignment *with* God Mind
to Receive Perfect Communion
in God Mind."

❀

Questing

"Questing individualized minds,
Seeking Truth
from The Source of ALL Truth –
God Mind –
shall Find
only Truth."

Guide

"Womb
of ALL Truth
is
God Mind.
Receiving questions
from The Returning Prodigal Son,
The Father –
as God Mind –
will Give Truth-Testimony
to Guide The Wandering Child Home."

Evidence

"Communion *with* God Mind
Testifies
Faith-*with*-evidence
but
only to The Receiver
in this Communion."

Open-Mindedly

"Only Minds
which have Communed *with* God Mind
Open-mindedly,
shall Know Truth's Receipt.
King without an Earthly throne
is such a Mind.
Kingdom-in-Heaven
is its Home."

❋

Blasphemy

"When individualized mind
in At-Onement *with* God Mind
Testifies Truth,
the word 'blasphemy' means naught
and only Serves
to Testify Truth."

❋

Evidence

"Desire to Receive Evidence
of 'The Words of Truth'
is
a by-product of a participatory society.
The Thinking Mind
is
The Participating Mind."

Leaving

"Leave
thy individualized mind's home on Earth
for thy God-Mind Home in Heaven.
Join
the Testifiers of God-in-Mind
as they are Awaiting thy Return.
Thou need not wait for physical death
as Heaven is Within The Mind of God
where Waits The Return of individualized mind."

❂

Heaven-In-Earth

"Yield thy will
to God's Will
and
'Heaven-in-Earth'
shall Testify Itself *within thy mind*.
Sanctified as God's Kingdom-in-Earth,
individualized mind in At-Onement with God Mind,
is Manifested through Desire,
Wedded with release of all fear and doubt."

Satan

"Asking passively thy questions,
Yielding to an Unseen Mind,
attracts fear.
Jesus of Nazareth
attracted this same fear –
fear of receiving error in Response.
Jesus Declared,
'Satan, get thou behind me!'
('Satan' Defined as *fears of individualized mind*
Transmutes itself
as error is no longer feared.)."

❋

As a Child

"'Becoming as a little child' (Trusting):
as ye Think
so shall it be.
'Testifying as children',
Suggests Testifying
as Offspring of thy Father-in-Heaven
without preconceived notions
of Father-Offspring Interrelationships."

Womb

"'Womb
of ALL Truth'
is *God Mind*;

"*The Christ*:
'The Womb of Truth
in humankind'."

❦

The Umbilical Cord

"Wedding
The Light Body of individualized mind
to its animal body,
is 'The Holy Spirit' (The Wholly Spirit)."

❦

Synonymy

"The 'Wholly' Spirit
Testifies
Oneness or 'At-Onement',
and
is synonymous with
The *Receipt* of Truth."

Spiritual Sustenance

"Attract
Spiritual Sustenance
through Testifying
TRUTH of thy Beingness."

❈

Inexhaustible Supply

"Individualized mind
only Serves as The Channel
of Love Energy –
A Channel
from an Inexhaustible Supply.
Mind of Free Will
Accept this Divine Channeling!"

❈

Ability to Commune

"*I and my Father are ONE*
is Defined as:
'individualized mind
in AT-ONEMENT with God Mind';
therefore,
AT-ONEMENT
Means
'Ability to Commune *with* God Mind
DIRECTLY
without benefit of a channeling entity.'"

Stillness

"Be Still
and Know
that I AM God,
and in this Stillness
I
will Come to thee."

❂

Inadvertent Opening

"Gates to the other worlds of illusion
of individualized mind
are opened *inadvertently*
in mind's Search to Understand Truth.
Attraction to God Mind
is the *only* 'Gateway to Truth',
and
through The Christ
is The Key."

The Psychic Realms

"A mansion of expression
of individualized mind –
'the psychic realms':
the opportunity for siphoning
past thought-forms from the ethers
are as numerous
as the siphoners who desire to siphon!"

❁

"Possession"

"'Possession' –
attraction to mansions of expression
of individualized mind,
which are script-testimonials
of past, mind-error-accumulations,
testified in varied script-formations."

Possession-Testimony

"Cause of possession-testimony
is the yielding of individualized mind
to previous incarnational history
which supplants
the present incarnational history.
This supplantation occurs
as an escape
into the nether world
of individualized mind cause-and-effect
because of trauma."

❈

Speaking with the Dead

"Attracting the thought forms
of those minds which have attracted
separation from the animal body
is simply that –
attracting thought-forms!
Communing with individualized minds
which have vacated the animal body
is not possible."

CREATION (BY GOD)

(See also AT-ONEMENT/CHRIST; HEAVEN)

I Am

"Because *I Am*
thou Art."

❊

Creation

"Creative Events were in Creational Scheme
Birthed *within God Mind*.
Birthing began and ended upon Idea Conception;
therefore,
Birthing was instantaneous."

❊

First Man

"*'Idea'* as first man,
beckons
Remembrance of *only Unconditional Love*."

God-in-Activity

"'The Word'
symbolizes Cause –
The Beginning of God-in-Activity
(which is The Beginning of ALL That Is).
This Word of God
is LOVE,
The Cause of Individualized mind
as Perfect Idea in God Mind.
With this Creation,
The Christ
Became The Son of God."

❋

Convergence

"Individualized Mind,
thou art Made
in My Image
and
after My Likeness –
It is Mind of God
Playing upon Itself –
Harmonic Convergence
of Mind upon Mind."

Ever Mindful

*"Be ever Mindful
of thy Birth
as
Perfect Idea
IN God Mind."*

Birthing Impetus

*"'DESIRE
is The Birthing Impetus
for Idea Manifestation;
therefore,
Individualized Mind
was The Effect
of Idea in God Mind Made Manifest
through The Desire of God Mind
to Express Itself."*

Self

*"God-Mind Label
for Christ
is 'SELF That was Created
as Perfect Idea
in God Mind.'"*

Expression

"Individualized Mind
was Created as Perfect Idea
through
Light Expressing Itself
as Perfect Reflection of Itself."

❁

Body of Light

"The Creation of Individualized Mind
was
In The Mind of God,
Which Created Perfect Idea,
Attracting unto Itself
a Body of Light
(Which remains The Perfect Pattern incarnate)."

❁

Life is God

"*ALL Life* is 'God';
therefore,
It is
of Idea Made Manifest."

Royally Gifted

"Enveloping our mind
in Its Own Likeness,
The Master Mind of ALL Creation
Royally Gifted
individualized mind."

❈

Right Hand

"*The Right Hand of God
symbolizes
'Perfect Idea in God Mind',
The Image of God Mind –
Individualized Mind.*"

❈

Jesus, the Christ

"*True* Individualized Mind,
as Originally Created,
is
'The Only Begotten Son of God'.
Jesus, *The Christ*,
simply *Demonstrated* that Sonship."

Developing

"The Perfect Idea in God Mind
is symbolically
'an Embryonic Light Body
Developing
Its Prophesied Mastership.'"

Recognition

"Mind
Recognizes
its Original Pattern of PERFECTON.
Birthed in WHOLENESS,
individualized mind
Recognizes
That which is *like* Itself
and conversely,
will *not* Recognize
that which is *unlike* Itself."

Expressing

"'The Birth of The Christ Occurred
The Moment The Desire
to Express Individualized Mind
(as The Effect of Parent Mind Testifying Itself) Occurred."

Cause and Effect

"Testifying 'The Word'
as *both* Cause and Effect,
John, The Disciple,
summarized The Relationship
of God Mind as CAUSE
and
Individualized Mind as EFFECT."

❁

Light Is God

"Understand,
'Light' is *God*.
Individualized mind
is Made in God's Image and Likeness;
therefore,
it, too , is Light.
This Light
is That of Which ALL things are Made."

White Light

"WHITE LIGHT
Serves as
'The Potter's Clay'
from Which Individualized Mind
was Created
in Its Beginning;
in The Image of The Potter
was It Made."

❂

Clay of Light

"Sanctified as 'Wholly Light',
Individualized Mind
was Manifested
from this Clay of Light
as The Light Body
by The Master Potter,
God Mind."

❂

The Cause

"LOVE
is The Cause
of individualized-mind Creation:
The Desire of God Mind
to Express LIGHT."

Envy

"Thy mind in God Mind –
My Children –
will never allow envy to exist.
No mind can envy another mind-
My children –
Heaven has Given all mind
Equality Everlasting.
Individualized mind
only has to Accept
this Divine Attribute of LOVE."

❂

My Eyes

"'No individualized mind
needs envy another',
Says thy Father-in-Heaven,
'all mind is Equal in The Sight of God Mind.
Mind which envies,
Sees not through The Eyes of God Mind.
Individualized mind with Spiritual Eyes,
is Mind in At-Onement with God,
ALL-Seeing'."

Receiver of All

"The Son
is
The Image and Likeness of The Parent,
God;
therefore,
The Receiver of ALL
Which is of The Parent."

❊

Born With but Not Of

"*Giving* and *Receiving*
as an Aspect of Mind-Function,
born *with* humankind
but not *of* humankind.
Coursing through all Mind
from The Beginning of Time,
has been
The Universal Pattern of Giving and Receiving."

❊

Two Aspects

(*Genesis* 1:27 "…male and female created he them.")

"Male and female
symbolize
'Giving and Receiving,
the Two Aspects of God Mind –
Creative in Function
through The Universal Law of Triplicity:
Giving-Receiving-Giving *ad infinitum*.'"

Androgyny

"Humankind is MIND
(it is not body);
therefore,
it is Androgynous
as God Mind –
its Creator –
is Androgynous."

❊

Genderless

"There is *no* gender in Spirit!
Understand,
in Spirit
there is *no* separation!"

❊

Christmas

"*Christmas*
is
'The Celebration
of The Birth of The Christ
which Testifies of God-*in*-humankind
as Humankind –
ONE Mind
ONE Body
in Christ.'"

Two Effects

"Angels and individualized mind
are
two Effects of the same Cause,
God."

CREATION (BY HUMANKIND)

(See also HELL; HUMANKIND; ILLUSION/SEPARATION)

Two Stories

(In *Genesis* I:26-28 and *Genesis* II:5-7...

"Creation testifies 'the beginning'.")

"The *first* chapter
Testifies 'The Beginning of The Son of God',
(The Christ or Light Body of all individualized mind).

"The *second* chapter
testifies 'the choosing of The Son to separate
from Its Parent, God."

❂

The Second Story

"In Genesis...

"The *second* story (of creation)
alludes to
'the animal-body incarnation
of those individualized minds
which *chose* to separate from God Mind
and enter the darkness of such separation'.
Separation is symbolized by
'choosing the body of clay',
the parent of which is 'lord god' —
the anthropomorphic god created by
individualized mind-in-separation *from* God Mind."

The Completion

(Genesis II:2 "...and he *rested* on the seventh day...")

"The *'resting'* Testifies 'Waiting The Return
of The Prodigal Son.'"

❂

God's Creation

"Nascence of ALL
is
in The World of Truth
Which Testifies
Perfect Image.
Think not Perfect Image Testifies humankind's creation,
for this is error-thinking!
Perfect Image
Testifies only God's Creation."

DEATH

(See also HUMANKIND; ILLUSION/SEPARATION)

WHOLENESS

"Understand, words which are synonyms for '*death*',
connote non-understanding.
'*Death Understanding*' is as follows:
'*Death*' is 'Returning Home to *Wholeness*
through vacating animal-body encapsulation."

❈

DEATHLESS

"Separation of the Spirit from the animal body is
not death!"

❈

FIRST DEATH

(*Revelation* II:11 "...shall not be hurt of the second death.")

"The *first death* occurred
'in choosing to incarnate
The Light Body of individualized mind *within* the animal-body'
(testifying of the separation of
individualized mind *from* God Mind)."

Second Death

(*Revelation* II:11 "…shall not be hurt of the second death.")

"The *second death* occurs
'as The Light Body of individualized mind
is Released
from the animal body of individualized mind'
Offering The Opportunity
for individualized mind to Return Home
to God Mind."

❂

Change

"There is
no death –
only
a change of form."

❂

Life

"This adventure
that individualized mind labels 'life'
is
that which God Mind labels 'death'."

GRAVE

"The 'grave'
of individualized mind
is *the animal-body
which it chose
for Earth-expression.*
'The Raising from the grave'
Means
*to have the Individualized Idea of God Mind
Released from the animal-body.*"

❊

DYING

"Only through dying
to Earth's illusion
do we have
Life Everlasting."

❊

JOYOUS

"Death of the animal-body
of individualized mind
is
'death of an illusion';
therefore,
be Joyous
as The True Self Returns Home!"

As Mind

"World of illusion
testifies death of the animal-body
of individualized mind;
however,
humankind as MIND,
Knows *not* death."

Welcome

"Thou need not fear;
The Self
goes beyond the animal-body.
Once this Self
ceases Its need of the animal-body,
It makes Its Way back Home,
and
God Gives
His Wandering Child, 'Welcome'!"

Opportunity

"God Mind
Defines 'death'
as the Opportunity
for humankind to Know God.
Death of the animal-body…
simply 'Releases The True Body,
The Light Body.'"

Suicide

"Suicide, no.
The Earth-expression
was the effect of Free-Will choice
of individualized mind.
Therefore,
think *not* that The Lesson
from this choice has been Learned
*until the death of the animal-body occurs
through OTHER occurrences
of cause-and-effect of individualized mind.*"

❂

An Illusion

"That which individualized mind
labels 'death'
is an illusion!
All separation *from* God Mind
is such an illusion."

❂

Going Home

"When individualized mind
decides to separate its mind from its animal body,
it,
in Truth,
is only 'Going Home.'"

Cheerful

"Christ, in Jesus,
Revealed thy Father's Will
when it was Testified upon The Crucifixion
of the animal-body of Jesus,
'Be of good cheer, for I Go to Join my Father-in-Heaven.'"

❂

The Veil

"Be Joyful,
as thy Loved One has simply Stepped through 'The Veil'
which separates this world of illusion
from
The World of Truth."

❂

Untethered

"Understand, *humankind is MIND*,
not body, and in Mind there is *no* separation.
Therefore, upon death of the animal-body…
with incarnated mind FREE of its animal-body tethers,
Attraction to MIND only,
is Testified."

Release

"Upon death of the animal-body
of individualized mind,
this mind
Yields to its Inheritance;
Attraction to Heaven-World Ensues
with Its attendant Phenomena."

❈

Love Abounds

"Ponder *not*
the next Level of Existence,
as
only Love Abounds!"

❈

Releasing

"Death of the animal-body
Releases The Body of Light;
however,
so will Attainment of At-Onement
through The Communion *with* God Mind."

FAITH

(See also TRUST)

Eyes of Faith

"See
as The Blind Man
with 'Eyes of Faith'."

Knowing

"Gnostics
knew God
as TRUTH
without direct evidence."

Blind

"The Reflection of God
is
Always Perfect;
only Vision
in The Eyes of The Blind-in-Faith
may See
such Perfection."

Gnosis

"'Faith',
The Thinking Mind's GNOSIS,
is in The Mind
of The Believer."

❁

The Rock

"Faith
is 'The Rock
upon which Spiritual Truths
are Revealed
unto humankind.'"

❁

Pearl

"Only
Act in Faith
and
The World shall be thy Oyster;
only
is Faith Capable
of Producing 'The Pearl'."

Cast Off Fear

"Cast off
thy mantle of fear,
and
Clothe thyself
in Faith."

Faith/Trust

"Yield
thy wedding of *doubt* and *fear*
to
Wedding of *Faith* and *Trust*."

⁂

Evidence

"Keeping Faith,
as evidence-attraction
testifies
naught."

Without

*"Faith
is
'Trusting
without evidence'."*

❊

Without Evidence

*"Yielding thy desire
for faith-with-evidence
to
Faith-without-evidence,
Testifies
Desire for Juxtaposing
individualized mind* and *God Mind."*

❊

Faith

*"Waiting
in Anticipation;
Bystanding
with Trust."*

Unseen

*"Faith
is
'The Evidence of things not seen,
The Hope of Return
to thy Father's House,
Testified
solely through The Christ –
solely through At-Onement
of individualized mind *with* God Mind.'"

❁

Always

"Yea,
I Am with thee Always.
As thou Step forth into The Light.
My Rod and My Staff,
they Comfort thee
all the days of thy life.

"All things will be Given unto all who will Follow Me.
Mind of humankind, Rejoice!
Thou will be Shown The Way;
have but Faith!"

Inheritance

"Only through Faith
in God's Inherent Goodness,
may
Spiritual Understanding
Effect Itself."

In Faith

"Remember only:
Truth
Manifests
in Faith."

Little Faith

"Evidence
is required
only for those
of little Faith."

God

(See also AT-ONE/CHRIST; CREATION (By God))

Cause

"*God*
is
'ONE
in CAUSE'."

❈

The Spiral

"*Alpha*
is The Beginning
of The Spiral of Creative Unfoldment,
and *Omega*
is The End Effect
of The Spiral of Creative Unfoldment:
I Am ALL
The Alpha and The Omega."

❈

Alpha and Omega

"*Alpha* means
'Cause of ALL That is Truth',
and
Omega means
'ALL That is The Effect of Alpha
or Cause That is Truth'."

The All

"ALL
is given many labels by humankind,
such as:
'The Great Unknown';
'God' in all Its many Names;
'Energy with Consciousness',
and in science,
'Electrical Impulses which Oscillate
as the Highest Frequency,'
That Frequency Known as 'White Light'."

❊

Essence

"*LIGHT*
is
'The Essence of God'."

❊

The Source

"*I AM*
'The Giver of ALL Light';
therefore,
I AM
'The Source of All Life'."

Waves of Attraction

"The LIGHT
is
'Waves of Attraction
to
Birth-Origin –
Origin of ALL That Is…';
only through such Attraction,
is
Remembrance of thy Holy (Wholly) Birth possible."

❀

Energy (1)

"Energy,
The Essence of ALL Life –
MIND
or
Energy *with* Consciousness."

Master

"Remember,
Truth of Mastership
is being
Omniscient,
Omnipotent
and *Omnificent,*
as is God;
therefore,
only God is Master."

❊

Synonymy

"*ONE* Mind,
ONE Truth:
God IS...."

❊

Is

"The *IS*
is
'ALL':
God IS...;
Truth IS...;
Love IS...."

Mind

"MIND
Knows *only Itself*
and
cannot be defined."

❊

Energy (2)

"God Mind
is
'Energy *with* Consciousness',
Imaged as The Universal Law of Love,
'As thou *Givest*,
so shalt thou *Receivest*',
the polarity aspects of electromagnetic energy."

❊

As Mind

"God
is MIND,
The ALL-Knowing Mind.
Think not
that God is Body;
this, too, is error-thinking.
God
is without form or substance.
God
is ALL-Giving through this Mind."

Unconditioned

"Giving is
'Returning in Oneness
The Giving from Parent Mind,
God Mind'
Giving from Parent Mind,
God Mind,
is 'Unconditioned Giving'."

Three-in-One

"God
is The One-in-Three,
The Three-in-One.
therefore,
God
is ONE with three Aspects:
The Aspects of
God *MIND*, The Giver;
God *LOVE*, Christ, The Receiver,
and *TRUTH*, The Wholly/Holy Spirit of Communion
between Christ and God Mind."

One-in-Three

"One-in-Three,
Three-in-One
(Effect Preceded by Cause);
Father
is
in The Son:
The Holy Spirit.
(*This* is The Christ
or The Light Body of all individualized minds.)"

❂

All-in-One

"ALL is ONE
through
The Christ
Means,
'through The TRUE Self,
or Individualized Mind
in At-Onement with God Mind,
That which is ALL-in-ONE
is
The Mind of God.'"

God Revealed

"Only *through* The Christ
is
God Revealed."

❊

Not Fear

"Think not
that God is a God of fear;
this is error-thinking.
God is
a God of LOVE."

❊

Attraction

"LOVE
Attracts
that which is like Itself,
unto Itself."

❊

No Entry

"Where LOVE Is,
darkness can find
no entry."

Love Is

"'Thou shalt LOVE thy neighbor as thyself'
Requests individualized mind
to relinquish its belief in separation
from its Parent, God Mind –
Testifying in its stead,
this Truth: 'All is *One*; All is *Love*.'
in Love, no quelling of hate is manifested;
LOVE is forever *in juxtaposition*
with ONENESS; therefore, LOVE IS...."

❊

Never Changing

"God
is The Same,
yesterday, today, and tomorrow;
it is only the Understanding
of individualized mind
which changes
through Revelations of Truth."

GUIDANCE

(See also COMMUNION)

SEARCH

"Ye become ceaseless
in thy search for happiness
if ye search from outside thyself.
Non-focus upon pursuit of happiness
but in its stead,
focus upon activities which give thee peace."

※

CONTRAST

"As *darkness* serves humankind
in seeing the effect of *Light*,
so will *negativity* serve humankind
in Understanding its polar opposite,
positivity."

※

FRIENDSHIP

"*Key* to friendship
is
being thyself *without* pretense."

Fear-Free

"Effect
'fear-free Be-Attitude'
by being 'in The *NOW*'."

❊

Advice

"Guard against advice
from those who do not know."

❊

Sacred Guidance

"Juxtapose
thy attraction
to Guidance-Testimony
with this TRUTH:
'Sacred Guidance
Asks only to be Given.'"

❊

Guidance

"Understanding:
'Attraction
to Guidance-Testimony
testifies
thy only prerequisite
for Its Receipt.'"

Footprints

"Be aware
of Destiny unfolding before thee;
be aware
of Destiny's footprints
in hindsight."

❈

Be Aware

"Be aware…
today becomes effect
of causes planted yesterday."

❈

Unopened Door

"Key
to unopened door
of happiness
is
Unconditioned Love."

❈

A Chance

"Each interrelationship
becomes
a chance
to *know* thyself."

For Another

"To Seek Guidance from God Mind
for another individualized mind
without permission of that mind
is *not*
The Will of God."

❂

The Deed

"Consider as error,
all testimony that condemns the doer of the deed,
rather than
the deed itself."

❂

Now

"*NOW*
cancels yesterday,
and
tomorrow is yet to be!
Be thyself each day
without thought of the morrow."

Silent Vigil

"A Guardian Angel
is in a Silent Vigil,
Guarding the aspect of the Oversoul
which is incarnate
or in other forms of darkness.
A Guardian Angel
is unobtrusive,
Guarding in Silence
the aspect Birthing its Light Body."

✺

Dreams

"Dreams become *Roadtrips*
Beyond *The Veil*."

HEALING

(See also ILLUSION/SEPARATION)

Perfection

"Understand this Healing Principle:
'In TRUTH,
only Perfection Exists.'
'Either/or' attraction
has become thy healing mode;
choose
Attraction to absence of duality."

❂

One Mind/One Body

"Only Remember this:
'ONE Mind,
ONE Body
in Christ.'
That which is testified 'imperfect'
through the animal body
is Testified 'Perfect'
through The Light Body."

One Mind

"Testifying both Cause *and* Effect
Jesus, The Christ,
brought forth
HEALING.
Oneness
Testifies
'*One* Mind
without separation.'"

Freedom

"*I Am without idea of illusion;*
I Am Perfect Idea.
Thou art Made in My Image and Likeness;
therefore,
thou, too art Perfect Idea.
With no idea of illusion,
thou art Healed!
This is
'The Truth Which will Make thee Free.'"

Transposing

"Yielding thy will to God's Will
through Affirming with BELIEF,
'I and my Father are ONE,
not my will
but Thy Will be Done',
Transposes the oscillatory frequency
of thy animal-body
with the Oscillatory Frequency
of thy Light Body."

❊

Healing

"Remember:
in MIND
thou art already Perfect;
Understand:
thou art not body.
(This Understanding only
shall bring forth Healing.)"

❊

Realization

"Questioning not 'Healing',
It is Done!
'Realization'
Becomes *The Catalyst*
for Healing."

Affirming

"Generate attraction
to animal-body Perfection
through Affirming *that* Perfection –
'I am God's Perfect Idea.'
Energy –
The Staff of Life –
will so Infill the Form that Mind Affirmed,
that the animal-body
will Reflect Its Testimony."

❁

The Shadows

"Thy Light Shines brighter
in the shadows."

❁

Light Body

"'I Am
thy Temple of The Living God,'
Says thy Body of Light
Manifested from Holy Light.
Thinking this Body is Perfect,
is TRUTH;
therefore Remember,
Perfection
Emanates from Within;
Desire this Perfection,
and It shall be thine."

Dis-ease

"Words that label dis-ease
are
of individualized mind only.
Thou thinkest 'dis-ease';
therefore,
thou manifest 'dis-ease'.
Attraction to health
is
through thinking of health."

Heaven

(See also AT-ONEMENT/CHRIST; CREATION (by God))

The State

"That which individualized mind labeled 'Heaven'
is The State
*of individualized mind being At-One
with God Mind* –
The Beginning of ALL Creation
in God Mind."

❋

Diffusion

"Yielding individualized mind
to God Mind Eternally,
Returns individualized mind
to 'The Right Hand' of God,
Position of *Receivership*.
Individualized Light Bodies
Diffuse with The Greater Light
of God Mind.
Individualized Mind Returns to Eternal At-Onement
with God Mind
in which ALL is Truth, Love, Joy, and Harmony."

Beckoning

"Guide the 'Remaining Ones'
as they Seek Solace.
'Correction of error
is to Understand TRUTH:
Understand,
as I beckon
thy Loved One Home,
this absenting
Yields to 'Becoming.'"

❁

Lifting

"Appearance of Heaven-World
is 'but The Lifting of the veil of illusion'
caused by
the encapsulation of individualized mind
within
the incarnational animal-body,
an encapsulation that distorted Truth."

❁

Opulence

"When first Seen by 'Eyes of Spirit',
Heaven Attracts
through Its Opulence of Love and Light."

In the Light

"Dwelling in The House of The Lord Forever,
Means
'to Be in The Light
Always.'"

❁

Celestial Sphere

"When The Celestial Sphere is Revealed,
The Opening will be That which has been labeled
'The Tunnel of Light.'
Attraction to this Light
will be
The Feeling
of Boundless Love."

❁

Tunnel

"To the testifier
of 'The Near-death Experience',
'The Tunnel of Light'
is The Passage-Way into Heaven;
this is TRUTH!"

The Promised Land

*"WAY to The Promised Land
is only 'through At-Onement
of individualized mind
with
God Mind –
The Christ.'"*

New Jerusalem (1)

(*Revelation* III: 12
"…the name of the city of my God…new Jerusalem")

"With Oneness of individualized mind
with God Mind,
Comes
'The Revelation of individualized mind's True Name,
its Spiritual Name.'
The Name *new Jerusalem*
symbolizes
this Revelation."

New Jerusalem (2)

(*Revelation* XXI: 2
"...saw the holy city, new Jerusalem,...")

"'The Return Home
of those individualized minds
which are in At-Onement *with* God Mind':
The New Jerusalem –
The World of God-in-Mind, Manifested of Holy Light,
The Heaven-World of God Mind."

❊

Jerusalem

"'The Tunnel of Light,'
Manifestation of 'Jerusalem',
Testifying The Birthing of The Light Body –
The Christ.
'Jerusalem' is the label for
The World of God-Mind Creation."

Angelic Hierarchy

"The Angelic Hierarchy
is 'Mansions of Expression'
of which were Spoken by Jesus,
The Christ when He Said,
'In My Father's House are many Mansions.'
(This alludes to Nascent Understanding of Truth
as individualized mind
Returns to The Light.)."

❂

Jacob's Ladder

"'The Ladder'
symbolizes
The Levels of Expression –
or Mansions –
of God Mind.
'The Rungs'
are Sanctified Expressions of Light
wherein Resides
The Angelic Hierarchy."

Mansions

"The separation
of individualized mind *from* God Mind
manifested the many 'mansions of expression
of individualized mind-expression.'
My 'Mansions of Expression'
are in Heaven.
The Christ Provides these Mansions
as Opportunities to Express
The Return to Oneness *with* God Mind."

Hell

(See also DEATH; ILLUSSION/SEPARATION; SIN/EVIL)

COMPLETE SEPARATION

"'Hell'
*the complete separation
of individualized mind from God Mind
as the choice of individualized mind.*"

❈

SEPARATION

(*Revelation* XX: 14. "and *death* and *hell* were cast into the *fire*.
This is the *second death*.")

"*Death* symbolizes 'the *first death*:
the separation of individualized mind *from* God Mind.'
Hell is
'individualized mind-in-separation from God Mind.'
The *fire* symbolizes 'Attraction to God Mind
which Cleanses individualized mind
of its error-in-separation'; this is the *second death*."

GRAVE

(*Revelation* VI: 8. "...and behold *a pale horse*: and his name that sat on him was *Death*, and *Hell* followed with him.")

"*Death* on the *pale horse*
symbolizes
'The Overcoming of the separation
of individualized mind *from* God Mind.'

"*Hell following Death*
symbolizes 'individualized mind
leaving behind its *grave* –
the animal-body.'"

LUCIFER

"When the separation of individualized mind occurred,
'The Bearer of Light'
became
'the bearer of darkness'.
So what God Mind Labels
'error of individualized mind'
(or 'individualized mind in darkness'),
individualized mind will *erroneously* label
'Lucifer, the prince of darkness'."

Duality

"As both error *and* Truth
cannot coexist,
may I Suggest
Testifying Attraction to Truth."

Humankind

(INDIVIDUALIZED MIND-IN-SEPARATON *FROM* GOD MIND)

(See also CREATION (by Humankind); HELL; ILLUSION/SEPARATION; SIN/EVIL)

Child of God

"Attraction-talisman
needs be:
'Truth of thy BEINGness' –
A Child of God."

❋

One in Idea

"Where God IS;
Mind of humankind IS:
ONE
in Idea."

❋

Relationship

"The Mind of God
is
CAUSE;
the mind of humankind
is
EFFECT."

As Mind

"Think *not*
that humankind is body,
for that is error-thinking;
humankind is MIND, and as MIND,
humankind is EVER-LASTING:
from ALL it came
and to ALL it shall Return."

❂

Needing to Remember

"I Make ALL Mind
in My Image
and
after My Likeness;
therefore,
ALL Mind
is in My Pattern of Perfection;
not One
is not so Made.
Mind needs only Remember
Its Perfection."

❂

Being of Light

"Thy *Inheritance* is
as 'A Being of Light.'"

Unconditioned Love

"UNCONDITIONED Love
is
'Seeing with Spiritual Eyes,
humankind as unembodied MIND,
The Child of God Mind'."

❊

Incentive

"No being is Destined to Effect
other than Perfection
(which Provides The Incentive to be Heaven-bound)."

❊

Corruption

"Understand:
The Christ,
The Light Body of all humankind,
yields
its Oscillatory Frequency of LIGHT
during incarnation
to the incarnational encapsulation;
therefore causing corruption
of TRUTH-Expression."

Incorruptibility

"Yielding
to The Incorruptibility of Truth,
will Testify this Truth:
humankind is MIND,
not body – and,
as Mind,
is Perfect Idea!"

Illusion/Separation

(See also CREATION (by Humankind); HELL; HUMANKIND; SIN/EVIL)

Illusion In Truth

"Illusion
'is being dead to The Truth
of individualized mind's BEINGness
as The Offspring of Parent Mind,
God Mind':
this Defines illusion
in Truth."

Without Basis

"'Illusion' Defined God Mind
is testimony
which is testified
by individualized mind-in-separation from God Mind
without Basis in Truth – Dream Adamic."

The Adam Dream

"'The Adam Dream' –
the dream world that exists
in
individualized mind –
which permits the illusion of reality
through its genesis
with other individualized minds.
The dream appears stable
because this world of illusion had been orchestrated
by individualized minds-in-concert
with other individualized minds."

❂

In-Concert

"The attraction
of the concerted individualized minds
in separation from God Mind
effect the seeming stability
of the world of individualized mind-creation.
The world of illusion
is *within* the concerted, individualized minds
in separation from God Mind.
This concerted error-orchestration
is embedded *within* the memory
of the gene-structure of the animal-body
of individualized mind."

Ego

"The smaller 'self' –
the ego –
knows only separation.
The Greater 'Self'
Knows only Oneness.
(The smaller 'self'
is
but illusion.)"

Return

"When one returned Home,
one became *At-ONE* with *TRUTH*;
therefore,
hiatus within The Dream Adamic
was negated."

STAR OF DAVID

"'The Star of David'
is manifested
with the *vertical* triangle
Representing The Ascension of individualized mind,
interfaced with the *inverted* triangle
of The Descension of God Mind
into individualized mind –
which symbolically *separates*
individualized mind and God Mind,
the separation known by individualized mind as
'The Fall from Grace.'"

❊

THINK NOT

"God is thy Father-in-Heaven.
Think not that thou art separated;
only thinking individualized mind is separated
from The Mind of God
SEPARATES
individualized mind from The Mind of God."

Confusion

"Humankind is Mind, not body;
it confuses *what it is* with *what it thinks it is*;
therefore, humankind remains in separation
from God Mind.

"Think not that thou art body,
o' individualized mind, for thou art MIND,
Made in My Image and after My Likeness,'
Declares thy Father-in-Heaven."

Separation

"Individualized mind
thinks it is separate;
therefore,
it has misplaced its Birthright –
misplaced in mind-in-separation from God Mind
*but not forgotten
in God Mind.*"

Body of Clay

"(As testified in the Holy Bible)
the animal-body is but a 'body of clay'
created by mind-in-separation from God Mind
(and labeled 'Adam').
This body of clay became a living entity
through individualized mind-in-solo
creating the idea
within individualized mind-in-separation
from God Mind."

❂

Blasphemy

"Individualized mind
usurped its Role
as it went forth to create a being
in the mistaken image of itself –
an image of a being of flesh –
playing a role Heaven never Meant to be.
Being, The Actor,
became being, the error,
a blasphemy to all that God had Intended
in His Wholly/Holy Wisdom."

The Serpent

*"The serpent
symbolizes
'The Fall from Grace' –
the separation of individualized mind
from God Mind –
the manifestation
of individualized mind's animal-body."*

❈

The Fall

"When individualized mind forgot its Birthright
at the time of
the symbolic 'Sin and Fall from Grace',
this mind believed
it was body,
and not MIND,
and the separation began.
Attraction to animal-bodies ensued."

Error Manifestation

"Individualized mind incarnate testifies the world of illusion;
therefore,
error may be manifested.
Such is the effect labeled 'illusion'."

❂

Age

"Age is
Foreign to Spirit."

❂

Error-Worship

"*The belief in the animal-body
of individualized mind*
is synonymous with 'the synagogue of Satan' –
worshipping the erroneous beliefs
of individualized mind."

❂

Temporality

"In Truth,
the illusion of the animal-body
is its *temporality* versus
the *Incorruptibility* of The Light Body
of individualized mind."

Genetic Imprint

"The animal-body of individualized mind
testifies *temporal* form
because of genetic imprint,
inherited from its animal-body parents,
transposing itself
upon The Light Body of individualized mind."

❊

Two Bodies

"The reproductive process
juxtaposes the body of illusion
(*the animal-body* of individualized mind)
upon The Body of Truth
(*The Light Body* of individualized mind)."

❊

Ignoble Raiment

"Wedding the animal-body
with The Light Body,
weds an ignoble raiment
with The Raiment of Wholly Light,
an abomination!"

Receptacle

"The fetus
remains an animal-body
up until the time
that an aspect of a particular Oversoul
would decide to join it,
and the animal-body
becomes the receptacle of Individualized Mind.
This occurs
during the first inhalation of air.
One mind, one body in juxtaposition
until individualized mind Remembers its Heritage:
The Mind and Body of Christ."

❁

First Breath

"The aspect of the Oversoul
which chose incarnation
testifies this choice
*with inhalation
upon birth of the animal-body.*
With this *first breath,*
incarnation is testified."

Sanctuary

"Until attraction
of the incarnating mind
testifies sanctuary for that mind
within the attracted animal-body,
the animal-body may be aborted
from the host animal-body
and not have willfully aborted
a living soul."

❂

Teaching

"Attraction to animal bodies
teaches individualized mind
cause-and-effect relationship.
As animal-body genes
are given in birthing,
there manifests various Opportunities
for attraction of those experiences
individualized mind may need
for soul Growth."

Race

"In
individualized mind-in-separation
from God Mind,
was ALL illusion created.
Racial distinction is of this illusion.
Individualized mind need Remember,
it is MIND, *not* body!"

❂

Reincarnational Belief

"The belief in reincarnation
was Testified to John
in the book of *Revelation*:
'and he shall go no more out.'"

❂

Involvement

"Reincarnational involvement
permits
individualized mind *the choice*
of Rejoining God Mind
through The Christ-Realization
or
to remain in the grave
of the animal-body."

Guarding

"Guard against
yielding to thoughts of separation
from Parent Mind,
God Mind."

❁

Reality

"The Reality
reposes
within the illusion,
awaiting Rebirth."

❁

Perfection

"See the Seed
of Perfection
in the darkness of error."

❁

Perfect Imaging

"Perfect Imaging
casteth out illusion."

Denial

"Testifying to the 'Withdrawal of The Light Body'
from the animal-body,
was The Appearance of Jesus, The Christ.
before His Disciples after The Crucifixion.
This Process is simply The Denial of the existence
of the animal-body."

Forgetting Not

"God in His Mercy
forgets not His Own.
No Mind is lost
only misplaced;
misplaced by its false beliefs."

Spirit/Soul

"'Spirit' is God Mind;
Individualized Mind is 'God Idea';
ALL is Spirit!
Yet,
individualized mind *believes* itself separate.
'Soul' is a word
for that which is individualized mind
AFTER *separation from God Mind.*"

Definition

"Ontologically,
'Spirit'
is simply *The Christ Self,*
and
'soul'
is simply *individualized mind-in-separation
from Mind of God.*"

Forgetting

"When thou forgettest
thy Divine Inheritance,
Remember,
kings of Earth
are mind-of-humankind creation,
but Kings of Heaven
are of God-Mind Origin."

❂

The Earth

"The Earth
is of God-Mind Creation
but
is seen as a world of illusion
through the eyes of the animal-body
of individualized mind.
The Seeing with Spiritual Eyes
will Reveal
its True Essence."

Spiritual Sight

"Desire
'Spiritual Sight'
with Right Motive,
and
'Reality'
will be Revealed!
'Seeing with Spiritual Eyes'
is Seeing Truth –
to See the Seed of Perfection
in the darkness of error."

❊

Peripheral Vision

"Thy consternation
lies
in peripheral vision –
the seeing of the view and not The Path."

❊

Remembering

"The Purpose of incarnational encapsulation
is yielding 'BEINGness' to darkness
so as to Remember The Light."

Supplantation

"'The world of individualized mind'
is *but an illusion* —
an illusion of mind-construct;
therefore,
what individualized mind has rendered,
Mind of God Idea can Supplant."

Seeing Truth

"When the world of creation of individualized mind
is Seen with Spiritual Eyes,
only Truth is Seen — Emanating as Light
from ALL Which is of God-in-Essence.

"The world of creation of individualized mind
is a world
Waiting to be Birthed in Light."

Peace

Ecstacy

"Effect 'Ecstacy of BEINGness'
by
Loving self Unconditionally."

❀

Patience

"Patience
gives forth
its rewards."

❀

Co-existing Peacefully

"Peaceful Co-existence
is Mind's Inherent Right –
a Gift from God.
Mind of God
Knows only Peace;
individualized mind
in Unison with God Mind
Assures that same Peace."

Freedom

*"Freedom
is
'Do unto others
as
thou wouldst have them do unto thee.'"*

❂

Conflict

*"*To Overcome
sympathetic joining of individualized minds
in conflict-thinking,
may I Suggest
Testifying this Affirmation
of Truth of thy BEINGness:
'I and my Father are One;
not my will,
but Thy Will be Done';
BELIEVING,
it will be so."

❂

No Fear

"Individualized mind
only has power over another
when such power is given to that mind!
Individualized mind
United *with* Mind of God
Knows no fear."

Protection

"When minds of darkness
meet Minds of Light,
I Make thee a Promise
o' individualized mind:
thou art Protected!
My Light
is thy Light;
thou need not fear."

❀

Trust

"Understanding
Way to Peace
is
TRUST.
Begin
with TRUST
and
all will unfold Divinely."

Prayer

(See also COMMUNION)

The Prayer of Jesus, the Christ (1)

"Our Father Which art in Heaven,
'Wholly'
Be Thy Name.
Thy Kingdom is Come,
May Thy Will be Done
in Earth as It is in Heaven.
Give unto Us this day Our Daily Bread,
and Lead Us into Righteousness,
for Thine is This Kingdom,
and The Power,
and The Glory Forever. *Amen.*"

❁

The Prayer of Jesus, the Christ (2)

"'Forgiveness
of sins (debts, wrongs, or offenses)'
is omitted from 'The Lord's Prayer'
because
God Recognizes not sin as 'The World of Truth'
is Perfect!"

The Prayer of Jesus, the Christ (3)

"Understand
individualized mind's belief in sin
testifies
belief in DUALITY
the world of creation of individualized mind
in separation from God Mind
AND
The Creation in Truth –
The World of God Mind."

❁

The Prayer of Jesus, the Christ (4)

"*In* Truth,
there is only Perfection!
therefore,
'sin'
is not Recognized
as Truth."

The Prayer of Jesus, the Christ (5)

"Individualized Mind
does not sin
as It is Perfect!
Individualized Mind At-One *with* God Mind
Knows
only Truth;
Jesus, The Christ
Demonstrated
this Truth."

❊

The Prayer of Jesus, the Christ (6)

"All sin (debt, wrongness, or offense)
testifies
separation of individualized mind
from its Parent, God Mind,
causing Truth
to be supplanted with error."

❊

The Prayer of Jesus, the Christ (7)

"God Mind
Knows only Truth!
Therefore,
why Ask God,
thy Father,
'to not lead thee into temptation
and to deliver thee from evil?'"

The Prayer of Jesus, the Christ (8)

"'Our' and 'Us' (of The Lord's Prayer)
correspond
to those individualized minds
Desiring Communion *with* God Mind."

❊

The Prayer of Jesus, the Christ (9)

"'*In* God Mind'
is synonymous with
'*in* Earth'.
'*In* Earth'
is Defined as
'*in* God Mind'
because
Earth refers to 'Spiritual Under+Standing,'
The 'Standing 'Under of Truth."

❊

The Prayer of Jesus, the Christ (10)

"'Our Father Which art in Heaven
Means
The Parent Mind of individualized mind
is 'Father' to all individualized mind
in At-Onement with God Mind.
This Fatherhood
is Accessible
to all individualized minds
which Choose At-Onement."

The Prayer of Jesus, the Christ (11)

"'Wholly Be Thy Name'
Means
Kingdom in Heaven
is
Kingdom is Wholeness;
ALL
is
Oneness.
Juxtaposed upon 'Name'
is
Kingdom in Heaven."

❂

The Prayer of Jesus, the Christ (12)

"'Thy Kingdom *is* Come'
Means
since ALL is Oneness,
The Kingdom in Heaven
is ALWAYS Present."

The Prayer of Jesus, the Christ (13)

"'May Thy Will be Done
in Earth
as It is *in* Heaven'
Means
Yielding thy will to God's Will,
Causes
'Heaven *in* Earth.'
Attraction of individualized mind
shall be
to its Parent only!"

❈

The Prayer of Jesus, the Christ (14)

"'Give unto *Us* this day
Our Daily Bread'
Means
through Yielding thy will to God's Will,
Oneness will Occur.
As thou give thy question,
thou shall Receive thy Response from God Mind.
'Our Daily Bread'
Testifies
Truth Received as Spiritual Sustenance."

The Prayer of Jesus, the Christ (15)

"'And Lead Us into Righteousness'"
Means
*Responses to thy Questions
during Communion with God Mind
will Lead thee Aright."*

❋

The Prayer of Jesus, the Christ (16)

"'For Thine is This Kingdom,
and The Power,
and The Glory Forever'
Means
ALL is."

Salvation/Second Coming

(See also AT-ONEMENT/CHRIST)

Coming Soon

"'Jerusalem'
is
Coming soon;
Jerusalem
Defines
as 'Time for Spiritual Re-birth.'"

❇

Slave

"All time
*is but an illusion
of individualized —mind construct.*
Humankind makes time its Master;
this obsession *with* time
makes individualized mind a slave,
mindful of only individualized mind's attraction
to the PAST and FUTURE."

❇

Returning

(*St. John* XI: 39 – 44 "And he that was dead came forth…")

"'Raising from the dead'
symbolizes
Returning to Truth-Understanding."

Birthing

(*St. Matthew* XXI: 12 "…and cast out all of them…")

"'Driving the buyers and sellers
from the temple'
symbolizes
Birthing The True Self,
The Christ Self,
by denying the phenomenal world
of individualized mind-in-separation
from God Mind."

❂

Finding

"He who *Finds 'Self'*
is
he who *loses self.*"

❂

Remembrance

"'Salvation'
is
The Remembrance
of individualized mind's Inheritance:
humankind *as MIND*
was Created in The Perfect Image of God Mind;
therefore,
Salvation Lies
in The Remembrance of that Perfect Image."

To Cleanse

"Receiving Truth
Cleanses
individualized mind of past errors.
When individualized mind
is Cleansed of past error and past false belief,
it is Reborn."

❋

Permitting

"Through Oneness *with* God Mind,
is 'The Salvation'
of individualized mind.
This Oneness Permits
The Christ (The Light Body) to Shine forth."

❋

Transformed

"Be as the butterfly…Transformed,
Identity Restored!"

As a Thief

(*Revelation* III: 3 *"...I will come on thee as a thief..."*)

"The symbolism of the *thief*
alludes to 'Remembrance of thy Inheritance
which may Appear when least expected
out of the dark night of thy soul's Longing
at The Time Known only to God.'"

❂

Understanding

"Individualized mind
is Coming Forth
in all its Glory
to Understand
That which individualized mind
has forgotten."

❂

Imperfection

"All imperfection
is
simply an illusion
of the Dream Adamic.
Overcoming this illusion
may be Accomplished
through Remembering
thy True Self,
Perfect Idea in God Mind."

Victory

"'Victory over self'
Makes all
the night of the soul
Reborn.
Ye who are Ready
for this Rebirth,
are ye of My Children
who Desire that Rebirth!"

❂

Cessation

"'Second Coming' –
*when the separation of individualized mind
from God Mind ceases to be."*

❂

Reuniting

"'Second Coming' –
is simply
*The Prophecy that Reveals
The Reuniting of individualized mind
with God Mind,*
INDIVIDUALLY
and/or
COLLECTIVELY."

Chaos

"'Chaos and turmoil
are symbols of Yielding the OLD
to Prepare 'The Way'
for the NEW.'"

❈

The End

"Prophetically Labeled 'The End of the Earth',
The Return
of individualized mind to its Birth-Origin
will Destroy the world of illusion
as known by individualized mind-in-separation
from God Mind."

❈

Giving Birth

"'Giving Birth
to The Child of God-Mind Manifestation',
necessitates, symbolically,
The *Death*
of the child
of individualized-mind manifestation –
(The Overcoming
of the false beliefs
of individualized mind.).'"

The War

"'The War
between Heaven and Earth'
describes
Yielding will of humankind
to
Will of God,
thereby
Creating Heaven on Earth
with Everlasting, Unconditioned LOVE."

❂

Wholly/Holy War

"Victory in The Wholly/Holy War –
The War of Yielding the will of humankind
to God's Will –
is Accomplished *individually*
by *each* mind that is in separation
from God Mind."

Saving Our Self-Image

"The Saving
of our Self-Image
will come from The Recognition
that we are the Phenomenon;
strange?
no!
estranged?
yes!
The estrangement came
from our separation of our MIND
which had been Made Whole."

Enlightenment

"When individualized mind-in-separation
from God Mind
Becomes 'Reborn'
through Transformational Enlightenment,
these Minds Testify The Desire
to 'Lead those minds
which remain in the darkness,
back into The Light.'"

Easter

"EASTER –
'Wedded Oneness Remembered';
death of the son of humanity,
Rebirth of The Son of God
(Testified as 'The Christ Within')."

❂

Advent

"Birthing
of The Light Body Within –
The Christ's Second Advent,
or
The Return of The Idea
in God Mind."

❂

Form

"Yielding to the desire…
to see *the corporeality* of The Light Body,
the attraction
of the previously occupied animal body,
testifies its form.
The Disciples
saw what they believed to be
the 'Resurrected' animal-body of Jesus,
when in TRUTH,
they saw the *animal-body form* of Jesus
Manifested as a Body of Light."

Mind-In-Glory

"Mind-in-Glory
Awaken
to thine Inner Knowing;
it is *not* too late!
The Dawn of thy Rebirth
is Breaking
upon mind's darkness."

❂

Born Again

"Dead to error;
Born again to TRUTH,
thy Mind
'Waits upon The Lord only'."

❂

Opportunity

"Opportunity
to Express Perfect Idea *in* God Mind
through
Choosing The Uniting *with* God Mind:
This
is to be 'Reborn in the Spirit' —
Prophesying 'The Second Coming'."

Not Alone

"Think *not*
thou art alone,
as this is error-thinking;
may I Suggest Affirming,
'I *and* my Father are ONE,
not my will
but Thy Will be Done'
as thoughts of separation occur."

❋

Freedom

"Separation of humankind
from ORIGINAL ONENESS
with The Creator,
is
only in the mind of humankind incarnate;
therefore,
Know The Truth of ONENESS
and
It shall set thee FREE."

❋

Mercy

"God
in His Mercy
forgets not His Own."

The Way Back

"When The Prodigal Children
Begin their Return Home, Choosing The WAY Back,
becomes
*a Decision Testifying Guidance
from The Oversoul's Tutelary Aspect*,
its Archangel."

❊

Remember

"Remember this Truth:
thy Inheritance
is as a 'Being of Light'."

❊

I Am the Light

"Understand,
I Am The Light.
(The Light is Waves of Attraction to Birth-Origin,
Origin of ALL That Is.
Only through such Attraction
is
Remembrance of thy Wholly Birth possible.)"

Baptism

"Think not
that baptism is to be of water,
as this is error-thinking.
'True Baptism'
is simply
The Desire
to rejoin individualized mind
with
its Creator, God Mind."

❈

Monotheism

"Wedded Minds
Yielding *only* to God Mind
will Know
the world of polytheism is dying
to Give Birth
to The World of Monotheism.
No more worshipping of the false gods
(which may be testified as 'worldly desires')
Worshipping in their stead
The One God of Truth."

REVELATION

(The *Revelation* of St. John The Divine I-XXII)

"Prophetic *Revelation* of God Mind
through The Mind of John, The Divine,
was Intended
for *each* mind INDIVIDUALLY
as it is Ready
to Find its 'Way' back Home."

❂

BE STILL

"Christ-Giving LIGHT
is
Desiring Birth;
Be Still,
and Know
That I AM God."

❂

ONE

"Remember:
only I AM;
therefore,
thou art ONE
with
The I AM."

Repatterned Mind

"This only Remember:
'humankind is MIND;
it is *not* body!'
The minds of humankind
may be Repatterned
to Image God Mind
and therefore,
Attract 'The Salvation' of those minds."

Age of Truth

"'Age of Baal Worship'
Defines as
*age of worshipping the false gods
of individualized mind-in-separation
from God Mind*;
'Age of Truth'
will Manifest
with individualized mind
in At-Onement *with* God Mind."

In the Midst

"Remember.
thou art in the midst of Salvation.
'Being in the midst of Salvation'
Testifies *thy time of forgetting*
thy separation from God Mind.
This forgetting is not yet complete;
therefore,
Remembering thy Wholly Birth
may Testify Itself only intermittently."

Sin/Evil

(See also ILLUSION/SEPARATION)

Original Sin

"'Original sin'
is
the decision of individualized mind
to incarnate
within the animal-body
of individualized-mind creation."

❊

Womb of Illusion

"Nativity of sin (error)
is
in the womb of illusion.
Sin
therefore exists
only in the world of illusion."

Yield

"'Sin'
is
*testifying separation of individualized mind
from its Parent, God Mind.*
When such separation occurs,
humankind as mind
becomes
testifier of the world of illusion.
Yield,
therefore,
to Truth,
and illusion ceases to exist."

Erring

"There is no sin,
only error of individualized mind.
Thou hast so erred,
but The Lesson
hast been Learned.
It is time to go on."

Error-Thinking

"Thou thinkest
manifestation of error
evidences 'evil';
this is error-thinking.
All error
*is attraction
to individualized mind only* –
this is 'error'.
(May I Suggest
that this word be substituted for 'evil'."

❈

Denial

"*Evil*
is
'the denial of The Inheritance
of individualized mind'."

❈

Lord god

"*Lord god*
is
'error, the creation of individualized mind
in separation from God Mind'.
This creation of individualized mind
in separation *from* God Mind,
receives its beingness from error only.
It is 'the false god of false prophets.'"

Give Forth

"Understand,
Forgiveness
Weds the mind of humankind
with God Mind
Testifying this Definition:
'GIVE FORTH
thy True BEINGness,
The Christ,
which Causes illusion
to cease to exist.'"

❂

Acceptance

"The error
testified by thee
Accepts Forgiveness;
therefore,
'Giving forth (Forgiving)
thy True Self'
Testifies
God's Will for thee this day."

Remembering

"Remembering error of the past
is
*to focus thy thoughts
upon that which was!*
Truth
Transmutes error!"

❈

Release

"I might Suggest to thee:
individualized mind remembers its past
so as to release it.
Thy past
is nothing to manifest shame;
the experiences of individualized mind
are necessary experiences."

❈

Fear/Love

"Mind of God
is Able
*to Transmute fear
into Love.*
It
Understands that fear
makes mind open
to the error of individualized mind."

Forgiving

"Children
shall be forgiven
without number
as thy Father-in-Heaven
so Forgives
His errant Children."

❋

Re-Directing

"Individualized mind
suffers long
from imagined transgressions.
God
Recognizes that such minds
are only trying
'to Find their Way back Home'
and that the imagined transgressions
are
only 'Needs for Re-direction.'"

❋

Truth Only

"Thou thinkest
thy errors
will continue to be itemized
within The Mind of God for all time;
*only TRUTH Exists
in Mind.*"

Judge Not

"God
judges *not* error,
as God Knows Truth only;
therefore,
that which judges error
is individualized mind
in separation *from* God Mind
(or 'Lord God',
the god of individualized-mind creation)."

Judgement

"Understand,
My Mind
is
The Mind of God;
therefore,
My Mind Knows no wrong!
The mind of humankind
makes the judgment
not The Mind of God!"

Punishment

"Think *not*
of God's Punishment,
only punishment
of individualized mind."

Cause and Effect

"Checks and balances,
causes and effects;
the seeds sown in hate
shall reap their bitter fruit.
The Wheel of Cause and Effect
Knows only Justice!"

❂

Code

"'Cause-and-Effect'
is the Code of Operation
in the Universe,
or 'As thou Givest,
so shalt thou Receivest.'
Therefore,
'As mind soweth,
so shalt it reapeth.'
(But the 'reaping of punishment',
shall be within the world
of individualized-mind creation.)."

Review

"'The reaping of punishment'
shall be
The Review of all misdeeds
so as to Learn
that which each represents.
'The *Review* of error'
of individualized mind
shall be Accomplished
with Unconditioned Love."

Giving

"May I Suggest:
Giving LIGHT
where there is darkness;
withholding anger
where there is ignorance;
Giving LOVE
where there is hate
and
Forgiving thy transgressions."

TRUST

(See also COMMUNION; FAITH)

Unlimited

"Without be-attitude of idea-attraction,
open door
to unlimited expectation."

❀

Full Sail

"Voyage
is now underway;
thy ship is in full sail…
therefore,
Captain thy ship with TRUST.
('Voyage is underway
with thy ship in full sail'
symbolizes
Nativity of thy TRUE Self.)"

❀

Total Trust

"'In *total* Trust
I Attract Thee,
Dear Father-in-Heaven',
so shalt thee Affirm
as thy choice is made
to Testify At-Onement *with* God Mind."

The Way

*"WAY to The Kingdom
Begins
through 'Becoming as a little child' with Communion Yielding
to Belief in Parent-Child ONENESS."*

✵

Trust

"TRUST
is based upon
Faith –
The Evidence of things unseen."

✵

Believe

"Not Trust
but thy Understanding of Trust
needs be Accomplished.
Trust
Defined God Mind,
Veritably becomes:
'Believe
without reservation
until Verified to the contrary.'"

Bystanding with Trust

"Genesis of fear is
in doubting The Word of God;
therefore,
'Bystanding with TRUST' Testifies God's Will."

❇

Anticipation

"Wedding
thy anticipation
with this TRUTH:
'God
forsakes thee not.'"

❇

Absence

(*St. Matthew* XIV: 25-26 "…walking on the sea.")
"'Walking on the sea'
symbolizes
Attraction *to* Truth
in absence of
doubt and fear."

Doubt

"*To doubt*
is
to open individualized mind
to error;
Truth will win – God is TRUTH."

Contentment

"As thy BE-Attitude
Testifies TRUST,
Contentment will Reign."

TRUTH

Expression

"Truth
is only
'CAUSE Desiring Expression.'"

✺

The Word

"TRUTH
is The Word of God,
and as The Word of God,
It Testifies ALL-Knowing."

✺

The All

"TRUTH
as ALL,
Knows ALL;
therefore,
It Knows
only Itself."

Knowledge/Wisdom

"Humankind
Seeks TRUTH as The Guiding Light
to Self-discovery;
Truth-Seeking for Its Own sake
without Self-discovery
testifies knowledge
not Wisdom."

Spirituality

"*Spirituality*
is Defined as:
'humankind's Search for Truth
beyond that sensed
through the animal-body of humankind.'"

Readiness

"Only The Mind
That is Ready
will
Seek Truth."

Wisdom

"He who Desires Wisdom
needs but Ask his Father-in-Heaven,
and
It will be Given unto him."

※

Astrology

"Stars guide astrologers,
but
God Guides The Truth-Seeker.

"Only through Communion
of individualized mind in At-Onement
with God Mind
shall Truth be Revealed!"

※

Revelation

"Yielding
thy mind
to God Mind,
Reveals TRUTH only."

Waiting

"Juxtapose
bystanding
with
TRUST and Anticipation."

❂

Fruit of Truth

"TRUTH
brings forth
Its Fruit
undeniably."

❂

Tao

"'Christ'
is
Tao;
Yielding to thy Christ Self
is 'Yielding to Tao'.
'Tao'
is
The Path to Truth."

Principle

"No Mind
was born without The Gift of Inquiry!
This is The Equality of humankind.
Created
in The Likeness of that Universal Law
of Giving and Receiving,
our Thinking Process
uses the operation of this Principle
to Open our Mind
to the Secrets of The Universe."

✺

Law

"This is the Law of The Universe:
'we Learn by first GIVING;
only through Giving do we Receive.'
'I am thy Teacher,' so speaks the question,
'only by going through me
will thy answer be received!'"

The Beacon

"Bring The Light of TRUTH
from under the darkness of hiding,
unto
The Beacon
of The TRUTH-Sayer."

❀

Tower of Babel

"Construction of the city and Tower of Babel
was legendary
without basis in Truth.
Legendary though it was,
it served as an analogy
to symbolize confusion
caused by churches yielding to testimony
of individualized mind-in-separation
from God Mind.
'Truth', The ONE Language,
was supplanted by error
with its resultant confusion."

Forms of Truth

"Truth-Nascence
is
when individualized mind is Ready
to Receive Truth;
Truth-corruption
occurs
as individualized mind is attracted
to self-aggrandizement.
Truth-resurrection
testifies the desire to remold Truth
for self-aggrandizement."

❀

Differing Guises

"Receiving *remolded Truth*,
individualized mind is subjected to
both Truth and error of individualized mind!
'Resurrected Truth'
will appear
in many different guises
throughout history."

❀

Sowing

"Sow
the Seeds
where the soil is Fertile,
Yielding thy will
to the Will of the Husbandman."

Defense

"TRUTH
needs no testifying
in defense
of Birthing Itself."

❈

Denying

"To deny Truth
is
humankind's choice;
Truth needs no defense."

❈

Belief-Systems

"Truth
is
TRUTH;
God
is
God
no matter the Returning Prodigal Son's
testified belief-system."

Truths of Birthright

"Testifying to The Birthright
of individualized mind,
Comes from Affirming The Truths
of that Birthright:
'I Am in God Mind'
and
'I Am Love'."

❁

In Truth

"ALL
is
Perfect
in TRUTH."

❁

Error

"TRUTH
will Know *no* error!"

❁

Truth

"Seeing
with Spiritual Eyes
is Seeing
TRUTH."

Fear

"TRUTH,
yields to fear
only."

✹

Fear Not

"Yield thy fears
to
My TRUTH."

Amen

*"AMEN:
'in The Light
of God';
The LIGHT:
The Truth
of God."*

❂

The Closing

*"'The LIGHT'
Which is God-in-Mind –
AMEN.
AMEN,
The Closing
of Communion with God Mind,
is in reference to this Meaning:
'to Signify Oneness
of individualized mind with God Mind.'"*

❂

Afterword

"Preparation of The Seed Bed, attracts
weeds or Crops of Sustenance; such is *the choice*
of the husbandman. *Amen.*"

Epilogue

The reader may wish to read four other books by the writer: ***Return to TRUTH*** and ***Vision for Education in a World Made WHOLE***, published by AuthorHouse; ***TRUTH Revealed*** and ***TOUCH...Not Necessarily Sex!***, published by New Age World Publishing. These are more complete bodies of work as Received in Communion from Parent Mind, God Mind (with the exception of his book *TOUCH...Not Necessarily Sex!*). His website <www.TRUTH-Beacon.com> contains that which has been spoken of as four *Revelations of Truth*.

You may notice a common contextual thread woven through many of these "Moments of **LIGHT**/Moments of **TRUTH**" as they are Responses to the writer's daily Communion question: "What is God's Guidance for my mind this day?"

Each response was the Guidance for his self-growth (his Growth into Remembering his TRUE Self as an Offspring of God) as he began that day. It was as if God Knew his question even *before* it was asked. The kernel of Truth in each Response may have been expressed in other ways, in other days, but each is recorded here as it was initially Received by the writer's mind in At-Onement *with* God Mind.

For those who desire to send written correspondence to the writer, you may do so by directing it to:

Lawrence Hall Dawson
15116 N E Graham Street
Portland, Oregon 97230.

BIOGRAPHY

Lawrence Hall Dawson: "Remember the Message, not the messenger!"

An educator: Formal education from the universities of our society; informal education from The Master Teacher beyond the world of humankind, God, his Creator. Taught within and beyond the classrooms of society from Hawaii and Oregon to Europe and Russia; an educator of the lay person; an educator of the Spiritual Seeker *outside the boundaries of organized religion.*

A presenter: First international audience with his Self-Quest/Self-Test Communicative Arts Program in Dublin, Ireland at the Fourth European Reading Conference. Later, Inter-Play Experiences (workshops) in Hawaii, Singapore, Sweden, and Russia based on his writings from his Communion.

A writer: Out-of-print books: **The Practical-Mystic: The Secret of The TRIPLE Spiral** and **The WAY Back-Home**.... Website: <www.TRUTH-Beacon.com>. Coming new books in 2005 from New Age World Publishing: **TRUTH Revealed...** and **TOUCH...*Not Necessarily Sex!*** and from AuthorHouse, **Return to TRUTH** and **Vision for Education in a World Made WHOLE.**

List of Titles

Ability to Commune, 102
Absence, 263
Acceptance, 252
Accepting, 73
Accessibility, 85
Adam Dream, The, 196
Advent, 239
Advice, 158
Affirming, 168
Afterword, 279
Agape, 90
Age, 202
Age of Truth, 245
All, The, 146, 267
All-in-One, 151
Allness, 17
Alpha and Omega, 145
Always, 62, 141
Amen, 279
Analogy, 92
Androgynous Mind, 91
Androgyny, 119
Angelic Hierarchy, 178
Anticipation, 263
An Illusion, 131
Astrology, 269
As Above, So Below, 23
As a Child, 100
As a Thief, 234
As Mind, 130, 149, 190
Atman Christ/Antichrist, 34
Attraction, 33, 65, 152
Awaken, 60
A Way Back, 64
Baptism, 243
Beacon, The, v, 272
Beckoning, 174

Beginning of the Light, 85
Beingness, 16
Being Meek, 39
Being of Light, 190
Belief, 81
Belief-Systems, 274
Believe, 262
Be Aware, 159
Be Still, 244
Birth, The, 22
Birhtright, 51
Birthing, 232
Birthing, The, 23
Birthing Impetus, 111
Birthing Reality, 24
Blasphemy, 98, 200
Blind, 137
Bliss, 40
Body of Clay, 200
Body of Light, 112
Born Again, 240
Born With but Not Of, 118
Bride and Groom, 20
Bride or Bridegroom, 20
Bystanding with Trust, 263
Casts Out, 70
Cast Off Fear, 139
Cause, 145
Cause, The, 116
Cause and Effect, 115, 256
Celestial Sphere, 175
Center, The, 94
Cessation, 235
Chance, A, 159
Change, 128
Chaos, 236
Cheerful, 132

Child of God, 189
Choice, 58
Christmas, 119
Christmas Star, 29
Christship, 21
Christ Star Formation, 30
Christ Within, 15
Clay of Light, 116
Climate, The, 53
Closing, The, 279
Co-existing Peacefully, 215
Code, 256
Coming Soon, 231
Complete Separation, 183
Completion, 32
Completion, The, 124
Conflict, 216
Confusion, 199
Consummation, 22
Contentment, 264
Contrast, 157
Control, 57, 70
Convergence, 110
Convergency, 79
Corruption, 191
Creation, 109
Cross, The, 47
Cycle, The, 11
Darkness Lifted, 14
Deathless, 127
Deed, The, 160
Defense, 274
Definition, 209
Denial, 208, 251
Denying, 274
Desire, 86
Destiny, 75
Developing, 114
Differing Guises, 273
Diffusion, 173
Dis-ease, 169
Discretion, 53
Doorway, The, 95

Doubt, 264
Dreams, 161
Duality, 185
Dying, 129
Earth, The, 210
Easter, 239
Ecology, 72
Ecstacy, 215
Ego, 197
Either/Or, 66
Emanation, 35
Embryo, 19
Emptying, 14
End, The, 236
Energy (1) 147
Energy (2) 149
Energy-Amorphous, 56
Enlightenment, 238
Envy, 117
Erring, 250
Error, 275
Error-Thinking, 251
Error-Worship, 202
Error Manifestation, 202
Essence, 146
Ever Mindful, 111
Evidence, 97, 98, 139
Expressing, 114
Expression, 112, 267
Eyes of Faith, 137
Faith, 140
Faith/Trust, 139
Fall, The, 201
Fear, 16, 54, 276
Fear-Free, 158
Fear/Love, 253
Fear Not, 276
Finding, 232
First, 57
First, The, 28
First Breath, 204
First Death, 127
First Man, 109

Flood (1), The, 4
Flood (2), The, 4
Flood (3), The, 5
Flood (4), The, 5
Flood (5), The, 5
Flood (6), The, 6
Flood (7), The, 6
Flood (8), The, 6
Flood (9), The, 7
Follow, 26
Footprints, 159
Forgetting, 210
Forgetting Not, 208
Forget Not, 21
Forgiving, 254
Form, 239
Forms of Truth, 273
For Another, 160
Free Will, 66
Freedom, 166, 216, 241
Friendship, 157
Fruit of Truth, 270
Full Sail, 261
Future, 63
Genderless, 119
Genetic Imprint, 203
Gift, The, 55, 75
Gift of Tongues, 80
Give/Receive, 46
Give Forth, 252
Giving, 46, 257
Giving Birth, 236
Gnosis, 138
God-in-Activity, 110
God-in-Mind, 45
God's Creation, 124
God Is, 18
God Revealed, 152
Going Home, 131
Grave, 129, 184
Growth, 71
Guard, A, 71
Guarding, 207

Guidance, 158
Guide, 97
Happiness, 74
Healing, 167
Heart, 94
Heart, The, 35
Heart Energy Center, 96
Heaven-in-Earth, 41, 99
Holy Grail, The, 95
Ignoble Raiment, 203
Illusion In Truth, 195
Image, 46
Imperfection, 234
In-Concert, 196
Inadvertent Opening, 103
Incentive, 191
Incorruptibility, 192
Inexhaustible Supply, 62, 102
Inheritance, 48, 142
Interplay, 88
Involvement, 206
In Faith, 142
In the Light, 175
In the Midst, 246
In Truth, 275
Is, 148
I Am, 13, 109
I Am/Thou Art, 33
I Am the Light, 242
Jacob's Ladder, 178
Jerusalem, 177
Jesus, the Christ, 27, 113
Journey, The, 56
Joy, 45
Joyous, 129
Judgement, 255
Judge Not, 255
Juxtaposing, 25
Key, The, 93
Knowing, 137
Knowledge/Wisdom, 268
Law, 271
Leaving, 99

Life, 128
Life is God, 112
Lifting, 174
Light Body, 168
Light Is God, 115
Little Faith, 142
Lord god, 251
Lost, 63
Love Abounds, 133
Love Is, 44, 153
Love Thy Neighbor, 44
Lucifer, 184
Manifestation, 74
Mansions, 179
Marriage, 24
Masculine Assignation, 30
Master, 41, 148
Mediator, The, 93
Mercy, 241
Mind, 149
Mind, The, 69
Mind-In-Glory, 240
Monotheism, 243
Motive, 38
Move Aside, 14
My Eyes, 117
My Pattern, 18
Narrow Way, 38
Nativity, 35
Needing to Remember, 190
Never Changing, 153
New Jerusalem (1), 176
New Jerusalem (2), 177
Non-Duality, 31
Not Alone, 241
Not Fear, 152
Not Forgotten, 58
Now, 160
No Boundaries, 12
No Conditions, 73
No Entry, 152
No Fear, 216
No Separation, 51

Ocean, The, 16
One, 96, 244
One-in-Three, 151
Oneness, 37
One in Idea, 189
One Mind, 166
One Mind/One Body, 165
Only One, 32
Only Receiving, No!, 87
Open-Mindedly, 98
Openness, 51
Opportunity, 130, 240
Opulence, 174
Original Sin, 249
Path, The, 17
Path of Return, 55
Patience, 215
Pearl, 138
Perfection, 165, 207
Perfect Imaging, 207
Perfect Mind, 47
Perfect Pattern, 48
Peripheral Vision, 211
Permitting, 233
Portrayal, 41
Possession-Testimony, 105
"Possession", 104
Prayer of Jesus, the Christ, The, (1), 221
Prayer of Jesus, the Christ, The, (2), 221
Prayer of Jesus, the Christ, The, (3), 222
Prayer of Jesus, the Christ, The, (4), 222
Prayer of Jesus, the Christ, The, (5), 223
Prayer of Jesus, the Christ, The, (6), 223
Prayer of Jesus, the Christ, The, (7), 223
Prayer of Jesus, the Christ, The, (8), 224
Prayer of Jesus, the Christ, The, (9), 224
Prayer of Jesus, the Christ, The, (10), 224
Prayer of Jesus, the Christ, The, (11), 225
Prayer of Jesus, the Christ, The, (12), 225

Prayer of Jesus, the Christ, The, (13), 226
Prayer of Jesus, the Christ, The, (14), 226
Prayer of Jesus, the Christ, The, (15), 227
Prayer of Jesus, the Christ, The, (16), 227
Prerequisite, 80
Principle, 271
Promised Land, The, 176
Prophecies, 4
Prophecy, 3
Protection, 217
Psychic Realms, The, 104
Punishment, 255
Questing, 96
Question, 87
Questioning, 95
Race, 206
Rapture, 33
Re-Directing, 254
Re-Throning, 59
Readiness, 88, 268
Ready, 89
Reality, 207
Realization, 167
Reawakening, 83
Received in Oneness, 90
Receiver of All, 118
Receptacle, 204
Recognition, 114
Recreation, 92
Reflecting Love, 45
Regeneration, 72
Reincarnational Belief, 206
Rejoice, 64
Relationship, 189
Release, 133, 253
Releasing, 133
Remember, 242
Remembering, 211, 253
Remembrance, 232
Repatterned Mind, 245
Reservoir, 93
Return, 18, 26, 197
Returning, 231
Reuniting, 235
Revelation, 244, 269
Review, 257
Right Hand, 113
Right Path, 54
Rock, The, 138
Rod and Staff, 11
Roots, 84
Royally Gifted, 113
Sacred Guidance, 158
Same, 27
Sanctify, 73
Sanctuary, 205
Satan, 100
Saving Our Self-Image, 238
Search, 157
Second Death, 128
Second Story, The, 123
Security, 52
Seed, The, 34, 61
Seeing (1), 40
Seeing (2), 40
Seeing Truth, 212
Self, 111
Self, The, 43
Separation, 17, 183, 199
Serpent, The, 201
Serving, 68, 70
Shadows, The, 168
Silent Vigil, 161
Single Eye, 23
Slave, 231
Sleeping, 59
Son, The, 36
Source, The, 146
Sowing, 273
Sowing Thy Seed, 38
Speaking with the Dead, 105
Spiral, The, 145

Spirit, 19
Spirit/Soul, 209
Spirituality, 268
Spiritual Heart, The, 37
Spiritual Sight, 211
Spiritual Sustenance, 102
Stars, 68
Star of David, 198
State, The, 173
Stick, The, 12
Stillness, 80, 103
Straightness, 39
Structures, No!, 82
Suicide, 131
Supplantation, 212
Sustaining/Maintaining, 72
Sustenance, 86
Symphony, 65
Synonymy, 101, 148
Tantalizing, 69
Tao, 270
Teaching, 205
Temple, The, 82
Temporality, 202
Testified Sonship, 28
Testify, 29
Testifying, 15
That Which I Do, 81
Tree of Knowledge, The, 62
Think Not, 198
Three-in-One, 150
Three as One, 31
Through Me, 42
Total Trust, 261
Tower of Babel, 272
To Be Like, 61
To Cleanse, 233
To Eat, 79
To Yield, 39
Transformed, 233
Transposing, 167
Treasures, 52
Treasures, 79

True Body, 35
True Foundation, 42
Trust, 217, 262
Truth, 275
Truths of Birthright, 275
Truth Only, 91, 254
Truth Testifier, 32
Tunnel, 175
Two Aspects, 118
Two Bodies, 203
Two Effects, 120
Two Masters, 67
Two Stories, 123
Umbilical Cord, The, 101
Unclaimed, 60
Unconditioned, 43, 150
Unconditioned Love, 191
Understanding, 234
Unfettered, 57
Unfoldment, 26
Uniqueness, 54
United, 44
Unlimited, 261
Unopened Door, 159
Unseen, 141
Untethered, 132
Veil, The, 132
Victory, 235
Vigil, 69
Wait-and-See, 3
Waiting, 270
Waiting Upon, 89
War, The, 237
Waves of Attraction, 147
Way, The, 56, 262
Way Back, The, 242
Way Back Home, 12
Wedding, 19, 22
Welcome, 130
When in At-Onement, 83
White Light, 116
Wholeness, 84, 127
Wholliness, 36

Wholly Matrimony, 21
Wholly/Holy Matrimony, 25
Wholly/Holy War, 237
Will, 53, 68
Wisdom, 269
Within, 15
Within/Without, 34
Without, 140
Without Basis, 195
Without Evidence, 140
With Truth Only, 13
Womb, 101
Womb of Illusion, 249
Word, The, 267
Word Spectrum, 71
Yield, 250
Yielding Not, 74
Yielding Permanently, 67
Yields Upon Request, 88

AUTHOR CONTACT PAGE

Directions: Please check the point-of-interest in author contact; fill out appropriate section; tear out this page and sent it to the following address:

November 1-March 31
Lawrence Hall Dawson
751 N. Los Felices; Circle W.; #M115
Palm Springs, CA 92262

April 1-October 31
Lawrence Hall Dawson
15116 N E Graham Street
Portland, OR 97230

POINT OF AUTHOR CONTACT

___ You would personally desire to arrange an 'Interplay Experience'/workshop presentation.

___ You would personally desire to arrange a presentation/lecture.

___ As a publisher of like-material, you would desire to seek possible publishing of my additional works.

Other: _____
_____
_____
_____
_____

Your Name: _____

Address: _____
_____
_____

Telephone: _____

PREVIEW OF AUTHOR'S WORKS

"www.TRUTH-Beacon.com" (Easily located with Yahoo/Google through a search using my full name, 'Lawrence Hall Dawson').

ORDERING ADDITIONAL COPIES AND/OR OTHER BOOKS BY THE AUTHOR

1. *For Whom THE LIGHT Beckons*
2. *TRUTH Revealed...*
3. *TOUCH...Not Necessarily Sex!*

(See: www.NAWpublishing.com; New Age World Publishing at 4071 San Pablo Dam Rd. #141; El Sobrante, CA 94803; e-mail: info@dubsarhouse.com)

4. *Return to TRUTH*
5. *Vision for Education in a World Made WHOLE*

(See: www.AuthorHouse.com; www.BN.com; www.Borders.com; www.Amazon.com; www.BAMM.com)